Career Launcher

Television

Career Launcher series

Advertising and Public Relations
Computers and Programming
Education
Energy
Fashion
Film
Finance
Food Services
Hospitality
Internet
Health Care Management
Health Care Providers
Law
Law Enforcement and Public Safety
Manufacturing
Nonprofit Organizations
Performing Arts
Professional Sports Organizations
Real Estate
Recording Industry
Television
Video Games

Career Launcher

Television

Amy Hackney Blackwell

☑Checkmark Books®
An imprint of Infobase Publishing

Career Launcher: **Television**

PN
1992.55
.H25
2010

Copyright © 2010 by Infobase Publishing, Inc.

Checkmark Books
An imprint of Infobase Publishing
132 West 31st Street
New York NY 10001

Library of Congress Cataloging-in-Publication Data

Hackney Blackwell, Amy.
    Television / by Amy Hackney Blackwell.
        p. cm. -- (Career launcher)
    Includes bibliographical references and index.
    ISBN-13: 978-0-8160-7962-9 (hardcover : alk. paper)
    ISBN-10: 0-8160-7962-5 (hardcover : alk. paper)
    ISBN-13: 978-0-8160-7984-1 (television : alk. paper)
    ISBN-10: 0-8160-7984-6 (television : alk. paper)
 1. Television--Vocational guidance.I. Title.
    PN1992.55.H25 2010
    791.45023--dc22

                                                          2009029548

Produced by Print Matters, Inc.
Text design by A Good Thing, Inc.
Cover design by Takeshi Takahashi
Cover printed by Art Print Company, Taylor, PA
Book printed and bound by Maple Press, York, PA
Date printed: May 2010

Printed in the United States of America
10 9 8 7 6 5 4 3 2 1

This book is printed on acid-free paper.

Contents

Foreword / vii

Acknowledgments / xi

Introduction / xiii

1
Industry History / 1

2
State of the Industry / 23

3
On the Job / 54

4
Tips for Success / 80

5
Talk Like a Pro / 101

6
Resources / 117

Index / 127

Foreword

I've been working in film and TV for the past 3 years. I majored in film and television at the University of Southern California, and from there I slowly wormed my way into the business.

I started way down at the bottom, working as a night Assistant Editor /Tape Vault Manager at a television promo house (the places that do the "Dr. Phil" spots you see on TV, among others). I worked there for about nine months, before I found a small step up to an actual TV crew in a reality home-makeover show.

I was hired as a Production Assistant on the reality show *Over Your Head*, and moved on to be the Construction Production Assistant. I worked there for approximately nine months as well, then through a contact I'd gotten while interning, I got an interview with an Art Department Coordinator to work on a full-length, though low budget ($5 million) feature film called *What Just Happened*. I worked there as an Art Department PA for about two months, until the film finished. From there, I moved on to be the Construction Auditor/Accountant on a sequel to *Get Smart*, called *Get Smarter*. The Construction Coordinator allowed me to handle his budgets and do all his paperwork and numbers, so I felt confident enough to interview for bigger shows.

After *Get Smarter*, I got my first big feature film. I worked as the Property Department Coordinator on *GI Joe: Rise of Cobra*, released in August 2009. I worked on it for about 9 months, traveled to Prague, and qualified to join the coordinators' union. When that film wrapped, I moved on to be the Art Department Coordinator on the TV show *The Office*, then in its fifth season. I finished that and during the break between seasons I moved into assisting my old Property boss from *GI Joe* on a Working Titles feature film called *Paul*, which shot in Santa Fe.

I work for the show *The Office*, where I am the Art Department Coordinator. A typical day starts at 7:00 A.M, when I hit the caterer for breakfast, and bring it into my office to eat at my desk. I spend most of my morning dealing with payment orders, check requests, and petty cash envelopes that I fill out, enter into my spreadsheet system that tracks how much we've spent on each episode, and hand in to our accountants and file my own copies for backup. Any activity that I begin is inevitably interrupted many times by phone calls, hot-rush requests from any of my department heads (I answer to the

Production Designer, the Set Decorator, and the Propmaster) which could be anything from calling a vendor to track down an important item we've ordered, or doing Internet research, to a menial task like making sure the fridge is restocked with bottled waters, or ordering more ink and paper for our printers.

The main characteristic of my job is that everyone around me takes precedence. I am there to in any way assist my department heads with getting their jobs done easily and quickly. That means I do a lot of dropping what I'm doing to suddenly assist someone. It requires the ability to multitask and keep multiple goals all in your head at once, without getting flustered when you're interrupted. It also requires the ability to deal with people diplomatically and professionally. People in the film and TV industry can often be eccentric, difficult, stressed out, and sleep-deprived. Usually, it's a combination of those all at once.Sometimes that makes interaction with coworkers rocky, and things can quickly get confrontational. It's an important part of my job to do my best to de-stress situations and interact with members of multiple departments in order to keep communication flowing smoothly and tempers cool. Sometimes, when I find myself absorbing too much of the stress around me, I need to step out of the office for a few moments to wring it out. Ping-pong games on the unused second stage usually serve as a great way to vent stress.

Word of mouth is the only way to get employed in this business. It's very rough, and sometimes harrowing. When a production ends, I often find myself near panic. You've got to call all your old contacts, remind them that you're out there, that you're now available for work, and then hope that a production will start with the right timing, in a location that's near to you, with the right pay, and that you know someone on it who can convince someone else on it that you're worth hiring. That's one of the reasons that it's critical not to burn bridges in this business, even bridges you swear you'd never step foot on again—because those might be your only connection to your next job, or they might know the guy who was going to get you your next job, and torpedo you.

Times are tight as of this writing in the summer of 2009, due to the downturn in the economy and the protracted disagreements between the Producers' Guild and SAG. More and more, productions seem to be moving outside of L.A. to other states with tax breaks, or even to other countries. But it's still a great industry to be in, and there's a niche for almost anyone in the business. A TV or film set is like a little microcosm of a city. We need to have all sorts of people on hand in order to make our productions run smoothly. Because of that, sets seem to have people who are specialists in just about every field—medics, animal trainers, business people, accountants, artists, stunt actors, makeup and hair stylists, costumers, caterers, maintenance workers, construction workers, editors, writers, technical support people, and so on. Basically, if you do something well, there's a good chance they could use your skills in some capacity in making a TV show or movie.

— Melissa Harrison
Art Department Coordinator, Universal Media Studios
Los Angeles, California

Acknowledgments

Thanks to Melissa, Marcia, Andy, and Steve for time and
wisdom freely donated, to Jennifer for her sharp eye, and to
Jon and Brent for many happy hours wandering through Venice.

Introduction

If you are reading this book, you are either contemplating a television career or already working in the television field. Maybe you want to be a producer or director. Maybe you would like to see yourself on screen, as an actor, performer, or news anchor. Perhaps your interests lie in design, and you would like to work with sets, props, lighting, costumes, or makeup. Perhaps you want to create shows and see your scripts made into reality. Whichever your preference, this book can help.

How to Use This Book

This book is meant first to help you decide whether you want to pursue a career in television (if you are still in the contemplation stage), and then to help you go about pursuing it whether you are starting from scratch or already working in the field. The chapter "History of the Television Industry" describes the development of the television industry from the late nineteenth century until the present day. It explains how early experiments with television considered both mechanical and electronic methods of transmission and describes the difficulty in broadcasting images with sound over the airwaves. After World War II, television stations proliferated across the United States and networks and advertisers hit on the symbiotic relationship that was the predominate modus operandi of television for the next 40 years. Cable and satellite changed the balance of power, leading to the current situation of confusion within the industry.

The chapter entitled "State of the Industry" contains statistics on the number of people working in the television industry in the United States, salary information, and prospects for growth. Television employs a fairly large number of people in the United States, but many of them are part-time or freelance. Pay is extremely good at the top of the field, but the vast majority of people working in television are not especially well compensated. The work can be stressful and irregular, with long but odd hours and occasional stretches between jobs. Unions play a big role in the television industry; if you want to work in the field for the long haul, join your union. Though television is facing competition from new media and from within the industry, there are still opportunities available for those who want to work in the field.

Turn to "On the Job" to find out exactly what jobs exist within the television industry. This chapter describes the main positions, from producer and writer to videotape operator, explains who might do well in those jobs, and describes some paths of advancement within the industry.

"Tips for Success" will tell you how to find jobs and get ahead. The main advice in this chapter? Network. Most people working in television find most of their jobs from connections. Television is very much a "who you know" industry. The chapter also explains in more detail how to advance in different paths, such as television writing or acting, and how to survive life as a self-employed person.

The television industry has its own language. Do you know what an "upfront" is? What would you expect to find if you went to a cattle call? Look to "Talk Like a Pro" to learn some of the jargon that you will have to know as a television professional. Finally, "Resources" lists a number of Web sites and books that can help you on your way to a career in television.

One last suggestion: Television is a field that changes very rapidly, and one that depends very much on personal connections. If you are serious about getting started or advancing in this field, you will need to look beyond this book. Stay plugged in. Follow networks' Web sites. Use the Internet social networking sites to make new connections and nurture old ones. And never stop trying. In this career, you may never get to relax and stay in the same job for many years at a time. But the excitement and personal satisfaction of working in television can make all the sacrifices and hard work worthwhile.

Chapter 1

Industry History

Television grew out of the development of photography, electricity, and telephone technology. People guessed that if it were possible to speak to people a long way away, then perhaps electricity could allow the transmission of photographic images over long distances.

Transmitting Images and Sound

Inventors began experimenting with television in the 1870s. The term "cathode ray" appeared in 1876, when Eugen Goldstein forced an electric current through a vacuum tube, producing light. In 1877, George Carey, a civil servant from Boston, made drawings of a prototype television system that he called a "selenium camera," which he suggested would let people "see by electricity." Other scientists around the same time were creating their own designs for systems called "telectroscopes."

Some of the early experimenters were most interested in using television as an adjunct to telephony, creating a way for people talking on the telephone to see one another. Alexander Graham Bell, the inventor of the telephone, was convinced that this was the objective of most of the scientists working in the field. He was so worried that someone else would perfect the technology before he did that he invented a device that he called a "photophone" and deposited it with the Smithsonian Institution in 1880, just to show that he had had the idea before anyone else.

The photophone did not go anywhere, but television itself was off and running. In 1885 Paul Nipkow of Germany received a patent in Berlin for the Nipkow disk, which used a perforated disk to convert images into dots and lines that could then be transmitted electrically. The 1900 World's Fair in Paris included a number of exhibits about "distance vision," the then strictly imaginary concept of watching live events from a remote location, such as watching a faraway concert at home. The first International Congress of Electricity was held there, and produced the first recorded use of the word "television."

Mechanical versus Electronic

By 1900, inventors were serious about making distance vision a reality. They pursued two different paths in their efforts to make viable television systems, mechanical and electronic. Some scientists worked with mechanical devices, based on Nipkow's rotating disks. Others focused on electronic transmission of signals, based on cathode ray tubes. Both methods resulted in successful television systems.

American Charles Jenkins and John Baird of Scotland both worked on mechanical models of transmission. In the 1920s, both of them succeeded in broadcasting the first television programs in their nations. These first broadcasts consisted of black silhouettes of people moving against a white background; no one minded the uninteresting content, though, because no one owned a television set. The electronic model also saw some success; Philo Farnsworth of San Francisco created an electronic image-scanning device called the "image dissector" while Vladimir Zworkin, working for Westinghouse, created an iconoscope camera tube called the "electric eye."

Television Hits the Airwaves

Aside from a few electronics nuts, the public knew little or nothing about early experiments in television. That changed on April 9, 1927, when Secretary of Commerce Herbert Hoover appeared on the air announcing the advent of the new technology. He said "Today we have, in a sense, the transmission of sight for the first time in the world's history." News of the broadcast made the front page of the *New York Times*. Over the next few years, several radio stations began making experimental television broadcasts, which were popular with hobbyists at least.

On the Cutting
Edge

The VCR Challenges Advertisers

The introduction of the videocassette recorder was a major event in television culture. Before the early 1980s, if you wanted to see a show, you had to watch it when it aired. Once videocassettes arrived, however, it became possible to record shows on tapes and watch them later. The crucial difference was that you could skip over the commercials. This drove advertisers mad. The rental of movies on videocassette presented another challenge to television advertisers; viewers could now use their television sets to watch movies while completely bypassing the networks and their advertising.

The videocassette appeared to be the beginning of the end for the mid-20th century model of television advertising. Later innovations such as DVDs and DVRs made it even harder for advertisers to force viewers to watch their commercials. Viewers used every technique they could to watch programs undiluted with commercials—a practice that, to the mind of television executives and advertisers—means that they are providing television entertainment to viewers for free. The arms race between advertisers and viewers has accelerated in recent years. Advertising agencies still vie to create the most entertaining ads so that viewers will actually want to watch commercials. Some programs place products within shows so that viewers cannot avoid seeing them (this is a practice that dates back to the early days of television). Ads personalized to viewers based on information about individual viewing habits may be the next step. This could be personalized with on-demand programming, delivering a customized programming-advertising package similar to the experience offered by the Internet.

RCA Struts Its Stuff

Television was not a real industry, however, until 1939, when RCA's president David Sarnoff introduced the first commercially produced line of televisions at the World's Fair in New York City. The highlight of the fair was the broadcast of a live speech by President Franklin D. Roosevelt, which was watched by several hundred visitors inside the RCA pavilion. Visitors also enjoyed visiting RCA's "television laboratory," which displayed Zworkin's experimental iconoscopes and the "Radio Living Room of Tomorrow," a mock living room that presaged the modern living room with its many forms of electronic entertainment devices. Visitors could even stand in front of cameras to wave at their friends watching on television monitors. "I was televised" cards were handed out to those who went through this experience so they could prove to the folks at home that they had been on television.

Although the RCA pavilion proved wildly popular, sales of RCA's four television receivers, available at Macy's, Bloomingdale's, and Wanamaker's in New York, did not take off. The units were very expensive, ranging in price from $199.50 to $600 —roughly $2,000 to $6,000 in today's dollars. They were not very useful. The cheapest models did not even come with sound receivers; their owners had to hook them up to radios to get the audio feed from broadcasts. In addition, there was not much to watch; General Electric's station NBC broadcast only about 50 hours of programming a month in 1939. RCA's competitors—including DuMont Laboratories, Westinghouse Electric, General Electric, and Ford Motor Company, also found sales of their models disappointing. Most of the sets that were purchased went to bars, hotels, and other places that wanted to attract crowds.

Fast Facts

Zenith introduced the first truly functional wireless television remote control, called the "Space Commander," in 1957. Previous remotes had either been wired to the television, or were wireless but did not work if sunlight got between the television set and the remote.

Coaxial Cable versus Microwaves

World War II put the development of commercial television on hold. Experience with electronics and broadcasting during the war proved that the electronic model of data transmission was clearly superior to the mechanical model, and from that point on television was an electronic medium. The question at this point was how best to transmit television signals. They could travel through cables or through the air, over the same microwave signals that radio used. Cable delivered a stronger signal, but required that physical cables be laid and attached to individual television receivers. Microwave signals were not as strong, but could broadcast their signals over wide areas without investing in physical connections to individual receivers; all a television needed to pick up airwaves was an antenna.

Coaxial cable—copper wire covered with insulation and aluminum—was initially the gold standard in television transmission; it was also used for telephone calls. AT&T began experimenting with coaxial cable in 1936, running an experimental phone line between Philadelphia and New York. The first commercial coaxial cable line was run between Minneapolis and Stevens Point, Wisconsin, in 1941. By the late 1940s coaxial cable lines linked many major cities.

Microwave broadcasters used radio waves to send signals from tower to tower. Western Union built the first microwave relay system between New York and Philadelphia in 1945. To make signals more powerful, television broadcasters installed klystrons, high-frequency amplifiers that generate microwaves. Microwave relay stations proved a cheaper method of transmitting signal than coaxial cable, so by the 1970s they carried most television programming. Cable did not disappear, but it was used primarily as a redelivery system to improve reception until the late 1960s, when cable television began to be more popular.

The Postwar Boom

As soon as World War II ended, electronics companies rushed to develop new television sets and stations sprung up like mushrooms. In 1945, there were only nine television stations in the United States, and fewer than 7,000 functioning television sets. By the beginning of 1949, there were 101 television stations across the United States. The FCC was so swamped with applications from across the country that it froze applications for new stations in 1948; this was meant to be a six-month freeze but ended up lasting until 1952.

What to Watch?

By the late 1940s there was finally actual content to watch. In 1946 NBC, with its sponsor Gillette, broadcast the first television "sports extravaganza," a boxing match between Joe Louis and Billy Conn at Yankee Stadium. The network estimated that 15,000 people

▼

watched the fight—at a time when only 5,000 households had television sets! (Lots of people crowded into friends' houses to watch the show together.) The children's television program *Howdy Doody* premiered in 1946. NBC debuted *Meet the Press* in 1947. *The Ed Sullivan Show* aired its first episode in June 1948; it continued to run through 1971, introducing a number of future stars to the world. *Camel Newsreel Theatre*, started in 1949, was the first daily news program in the United States. Fans of the arts could watch live theatrical productions of plays by Arthur Miller and other playwrights on *Kraft Television Theater* or *Studio One*.

Advertising and Television Join Forces

Advertisers embraced television in the late 1940s. It seemed clear that television was about to explode, and would be an ideal medium for reaching thousands of viewers at once. Texaco, B.F. Goodrich, and other companies all put their money behind shows and in return got their names on television through having their names added to program titles and their products placed in the shows themselves. Lincoln-Mercury sponsored *The Ed Sullivan Show*. In 1949, the United States Department of Commerce issued a report on television advertising in which it equated the combination of moving pictures, sound, and immediacy with a personal sales solicitation. By 1950 sponsors were abandoning radio stations in droves and putting their support behind television instead.

This enthusiastic support by advertisers is what made it possible for television networks to broadcast their content free of charge. Television stations, like radio stations before them, quickly came to depend on advertisers for their support. Critics disliked advertising because they believed it dictated the content of television programs, it encouraged rampant consumerism, and because children were unable to tell the difference between advertisements and facts. The National Association of Radio and Television Broadcasters passed a Television Code in 1952 that specified allowable content; much of this code was devoted to advertising. Over the next 50 years, many other types of advertisements became the subject of criticism or concern, including negative political advertisements, cigarette commercials, and advertisements for sugar cereals.

Today advertisers consider television commercials an extremely effective method of reaching markets, and television networks routinely charge extremely high prices for airtime during popular shows such as the Super Bowl. This effectiveness is despite the preferences of viewers, most of whom dislike watching commercials. In a 1967 survey, two-thirds of respondents said that they would prefer to watch television without commercials.

For decades viewers had put up with commercials to see their shows, but modern viewers have more strategies to avoid advertising. The challenge advertisers face is reaching viewers in a television environment with multiple channels, remotes, and TiVo, all of which make it easy for viewers to avoid seeing the commercials for which companies pay so much money. Product placements, embedded ads, and other techniques allow advertisers to work around viewer behavior.

Development of the Networks

Television networks arose out of older radio networks and for many years used a model similar to that of radio. Networks were large national companies that produced programming. They broadcast this material over series of antennae and through stations that were owned by local affiliates. In order for a station to broadcast its shows in a particular area, it needed a local station affiliate. The FCC sold rights to buy local stations, doing its best to spread network coverage evenly. If the FCC would not sell a station to a network, that network could not broadcast anything in the station's area.

Between the mid-1940s and the mid-1970s, television programming was dominated by three major networks: NBC, ABC, and CBS. One other network, DuMont, attempted to gain a foothold and failed by the mid-1950s. This three-network domination, the result of restrictive policies by the FCC, pressure from advertisers, and aggressive defense of turf by local stations, was the reason that most homes were stuck with just four channels (including public television) until the mid-1970s.

NBC

NBC, the National Broadcasting Company, was formed in 1926 by the Radio Corporation of America (RCA). At the time, NBC was jointly owned by RCA, General Electric, and Westinghouse. NBC ran radio networks across the United States. Its two main divisions were the Blue Network and the Red Network. In 1939 the FCC determined that NBC had created a monopoly in radio broadcasting and ordered NBC to divest itself of one of its networks. In 1940, NBC divided itself into two companies. After several years, court appeals, and sales, the two companies were known as NBC and ABC (for American Broadcasting Company).

CBS

CBS started out as the Columbia Broadcasting System, a group of 16 radio stations purchased by William Paley in 1928. CBS was the dominant radio network in the United States for much of the 1950s and 1960s.

CBS was slow to enter television. It began experimenting with limited broadcasts in the New York area in the late 1930s. During the late 1940s NBC dominated television. CBS was experimenting with color television systems around this time, but their technology did not work over the black-and-white standards pioneered by RCA and NBC, which prevented the company from entering the television field. In 1950 CBS started buying television stations in major cities outside New York.

CBS soon became quite successful at television, dominating the airwaves in the mid-1950s. Lucille Ball's comedy *I Love Lucy* began running in 1951, and continued to appear until 1960. It was the most-watched show in the country for several seasons. The show developed the pattern for future television sitcoms: a complete set with multiple cameras set in a sound stage, a small cast of regular characters, a lack of character development, and zany plots that could be quickly resolved. Although the shows were broadcast live, Desi Arnaz, Ball's husband and co-star, insisted that the shows be recorded on film as well so that stations without live broadcasts could still broadcast high-quality images. (Arnaz and Ball's production company covered the cost of the film and retained the rights to the films, which made them very wealthy after re-runs of *I Love Lucy* began to appear.) Arnaz also insisted on accommodating a live audience inside the sound stage during filming of the show. The success of *I Love Lucy* and other shows put CBS at the top of television ratings by 1955, a slot it maintained until the mid-1970s.

ABC

ABC's owner, Edward Noble, who also owned Life Savers candy and Rexall drugstores, started out by purchasing hit radio shows.

It was evident, however, that in order to succeed in broadcasting, ABC would have to enter the world of television. In 1947 it requested licenses to broadcast on television channel 7 in five cities where it already owned radio stations. ABC went on the air in Philadelphia, Washington, Detroit, Chicago, San Francisco, Los Angeles, and New York in 1948 and 1949. At that point, ABC's expansion stopped for several years while the FCC froze applications for new stations as it sorted out its technical standards. ABC, as the third network to hit the scene, was at a disadvantage to NBC and CBS, which had more stations in more markets. ABC nearly went bankrupt by 1951. The company was saved by a merger with Paramount in 1953. With Paramount's resources behind it, ABC finally had the financial resources to compete with CBS and NBC. ABC introduced hit series including *Disneyland*, produced by Walt Disney, *The Adventures of Ozzie and Harriet*, and *Leave It To Beaver*. By the 1960s, ABC's programming was especially popular with younger viewers.

DuMont

DuMont was the world's first commercial television network, since NBC and ABC got their starts as radio networks. DuMont was founded in 1945 by Allen B. DuMont, owner of DuMont Laboratories, a manufacturer of television equipment. The network began broadcasting regular programs in 1946.DuMont was known for its creative programming, featuring Broadway shows, early sitcoms and soap operas, and the devotional program *Life is Worth Living*. In the early 1950s DuMont pioneered the then unusual practice of selling a show's advertising to a number of companies instead of having a single sponsor for every show. This later became standard practice throughout the industry.

DuMont never had much money to spend, and had trouble getting FCC permission to acquire new stations. When ABC merged with Paramount in 1953 DuMont lost all hope of becoming a rival to the two major networks. ABC attempted to buy the network, but Paramount, a long-standing investor in DuMont Laboratories, refused to permit the merger. In 1956 DuMont Television Network was shut down. Some of DuMont's programming was stored in a warehouse for a number of years, but most of it was destroyed in the 1970s, leaving DuMont to be largely forgotten by everyone but a few television history buffs.

Educational Programming

Educational programming was provided by National Educational Television (NET), a network founded in 1952. NET, supported by a grant from the Ford Foundation, at first just distributed educational programs produced by local television stations. It did not produce its own content. During the mid-1950s the organization began making its own programs, particularly lengthy interviews with scholars and experts. (The popular children's program *Mister Rogers' Neighborhood*, started out on NET.) In the early 1960s, NET began importing content from the British Broadcasting Corporation (BBC) and making documentaries exploring social issues such as racism. Though many admired this work, it also opened up the network to accusations of liberal bias.

In 1966 the Ford Foundation began withdrawing funding for NET, endangering the future of public television. The United States government saved public television by creating the Corporation for Public Broadcasting (CPB) in 1967; the CPB opened its own television station, the Public Broadcasting Service (PBS) in 1969. NET continued to produce its controversial documentaries until 1970, when the CPB and the Ford Foundation insisted that NET merge with the New Jersey public television station WNDT-TV and stop producing controversial programming or be shut down.

PBS created a distribution model in which local public television stations schedule their own programming, paying for shows distributed by PBS. PBS did not and does not produce its own content. Instead, individual member stations and other entities produce shows and offer them to PBS for distribution. Many member stations are owned and operated as nonprofits. This model has meant that since its inception, public television has had to constantly solicit financial support from viewers.

License to Broadcast: Ask the FCC

The Federal Communication Commission (FCC) was established in 1934 as a successor to the Federal Radio Commission. The FCC's duties include regulating interstate telecommunications through wire, cable, or satellite, and all use of the radio waves for radio and television broadcasting.

During the early days of television, the FCC had to figure out how to issue permits to new stations in such a way that every station had enough space in the airwaves; if stations were too close to each other, their broadcasts interfered with one another. Between 1947 and 1948 so many stations opened that interference became a real problem. The FCC's solution was to put a freeze on permits for new station licenses in 1948. This freeze lasted for four years.

Part of the problem at the time was that television manufacturers were debating which spectrum of radio waves to use for broadcasts. There are two ranges of waves commonly used for transmission of information. The very high frequency (VHF) range is between 30 megahertz and 300 megahertz. The ultra high frequency (UHF) range is between 300 and 3,000 megahertz. Both of these ranges can be picked up with antennas. UHF waves are smaller than VHF waves, so a smaller antenna will pick them up. On the other hand, VHF waves are not as easily blocked by buildings as UHF waves.

In the 1940s, the FCC was assigning stations only in the VHF range, with the support of RCA and NBC. CBS wanted the FCC to allow stations to broadcast in the UHF range as well. During the freeze on permits, the FCC and network representatives debated the merits of allocating channels to UHF and color television technology. It became clear that there were not enough VHF channels to accommodate the entire country. The FCC had designated 12 channels, numbers 2 through 13, as VHF television stations, and had to distribute those among markets in such a way that they did not interfere with one another. Adding UHF channels would greatly increase the number of available channels, although UHF broadcasts were not yet strong enough to reach large areas.

By 1952 the country was already running out of channels on VHF. The FCC ended the freeze and started issuing permits for new television stations. It allowed a mixture of UHF and VHF stations and set aside some channels for educational programming. In 1952, the FCC announced in the Sixth Report and Order that it would therefore open up UHF channels to television broadcasting. This created 70 new channels, 14 through 83. It also granted most television markets three VHF channels.

Developing Technologies

Following the establishment of the major television networks and the creation of new channels, the television-viewing experience was improved with several technological breakthroughs.

Color Television

Although networks wanted to make color a reality and had been experimenting with it for years, television from the 1940s though the 1960s was mostly black and white. Almost all television sets in those days only displayed black and white images, and most shows were shot in black and white.

In 1946 Peter Goldmark of CBS developed a system of producing color pictures by having a color wheel spin in front of a cathode ray tube. Color television was first used to broadcast medical operations performed in Pennsylvania and Atlantic City hospitals to the convention center in Atlantic City. Visitors flocked to these broadcasts, which became notorious for the number of viewers who fainted upon seeing full-color medical procedures. This technology, however, failed to catch on.

CBS and RCA wanted to use different systems for generating color, which complicated matters with the FCC. The FCC chose the CBS system as the official United States color broadcasting standard in 1950. CBS broadcast the first color television program in 1951, but almost none of the sets in the United States could receive images; viewers saw only a blank screen. By 1951, a rival system championed by RCA proved more effective, and in 1953 CBS dropped its plans for its own system. At that point the FCC gave its permission to manufacturers to make color television receivers.

The first color televisions were offered for sale in 1954. The three networks all began producing some color content, but it was not until 1966 that almost all programming was produced in color, and black and white televisions continued to outsell color sets until 1972.

Distributing Programs

In the early days of television, most programs were either broadcast live or distributed by means of kinescope recordings. A kinescope was basically a film camera that shot images from a television monitor. The four networks set up kinescope recording facilities, where they recorded programs and shipped the films out to their affiliate networks. Often a show would be performed and broadcast live in New York and shown later in California on kinescope. The result was typically jerky and fuzzy, and coordinating sound was difficult, but this was the only method available for recording and replaying television programs until videotape was introduced in 1956. Even then networks continued to use kinescopes until 1969.

The introduction of videotape in 1956 made it possible to produce television programs anywhere. Up to that point, most television programs were produced in New York. Afterward, although most news and business programming production remained on the East Coast, the production of artistic and dramatic programming moved to Hollywood. Today both New York and Los Angeles are major centers of television production. Most major networks maintain offices in both locations. The old patterns hold true, though with many exceptions. For the most part, dramatic shows are produced in Los Angeles, where there is considerable overlap between the television and film industries. Many people who work in television today have held jobs on both film and television productions because the skills needed to work in both industries are essentially the same. New York is also the home of a number of major television productions, both serious programming such as news and business and comedy productions such as *Saturday Night Live*. Although some major networks are based in other cities (CNN in Atlanta is a big one), television professionals today give the same advice to newcomers that they did 50 years ago: if you want to work in television, move to New York or Los Angeles.

Satellite and Cable

During the 1960s and 1970s almost every American television set used an antenna to pick up the three commercial networks and PBS. Sets had double dials, allowing viewers to access both VHF and UHF channels. Many broadcasters wanted to branch into alternate means of transmitting signals such as cable, but they were prevented by FCC restrictions, which did not allow competition with local advertising-driving networks.

Cable developed slowly during the mid-20th century. The networks did not like the idea of cable companies competing with them, particularly since cable could provide signals from much farther away than local network stations could. During the 1960s the FCC restricted the right of cable systems to provide services. Cable companies could offer only broadcasts of sporting events, movies, and syndicated programs. The FCC loosened these restrictions in the early 1970s, paving the way for the explosive growth of cable television.

In the 1980s, though, cable took off. Several new cable stations appeared in the late 1970s and early 1980s. The movie channel Showtime debuted in 1978, the sports network ESPN arrived in 1979, and CNN and MTV both began operation in 1980. The Home Shopping Network was launched in 1982. Viewers suddenly had the opportunity to see shows without as many commercials and often with better reception than they received over the air. People were apparently willing to pay for these channels, and to put up with installation of cable and boxes. For many years cable access was restricted to certain areas; cable companies could not run cable to every single residence, so viewers in remote regions were stuck with the networks, or, later, satellite dishes.

Fast Facts

CBS gained a certain amount of notoriety when it broadcast a production of H.G. Wells' *The War of the Worlds* on the radio in 1938. In this radio play, Martians invade the earth. Listeners failed to realize that they were listening to a play being read, and thought invaders from Mars really had arrived in New Jersey.

HBO: A Cable Success Story

Home Box Office, or HBO, was one of the first cable companies. Long Island businessman Charles Dolan concocted the idea for a pay-cable channel in 1971. At the time, programming on the three major networks, ABC, CBS, and NBC, accounted for about 97 percent of the television watched in the United States; public television made up most of the rest. Cable television systems, called Community Antenna Television, had been around since the late 1940s, but they were mainly in rural areas where television signals were nonexistent due to mountains or distance from towers.

Dolan thought that people might enjoy the opportunity to watch programming uninterrupted by commercials, particularly uncensored long movies, and guessed that they would be willing to pay for this service. He calculated that if enough viewers paid for his network, he would not need to attract a vast number of advertisers to cover his expenses in exchange for commercial time. Dolan set up HBO in 1972. That November HBO broadcast its first film, *Sometimes A Great Notion*, to 365 houses in Wilkes-Barre, Pennsylvania.

HBO grew slowly at first, and the networks were inclined to dismiss it. But it soon became apparent that people were indeed willing to pay for good programming, particularly for the satellite broadcasts in which the company specialized. Satellite transmission was a major factor in the growth of cable television in the 1970s. Satellite transmissions could be broadcast live only over cable networks; broadcast networks, on the other hand, had to wait for tapes of events to be flown to them, so viewers had to wait a day or two to see them. Dolan made a practice of using the proceeds from subscriptions to purchase the rights to satellite broadcasts of major sporting events. HBO cemented its reputation for providing the most immediate content in 1975, when the company purchased the rights to the boxing match in the Philippines between Muhammad Ali and Joe Frazier, known as "The Thrilla in Manila." This widely anticipated fight, intended to decide once and for all who was the world heavyweight champion, was broadcast live by HBO.

During the 1980s, HBO became a major industry player, airing major concerts by stars such as Barbra Streisand and Bette Midler. It was in the mid-1980s that company president Michael Fuchs announced that HBO would begin creating its own content. The television industry initially scoffed at this plan, and detractors suggested that HBO should stick to what it knew, live broadcasts of sporting events and concerts and movies. Fuchs, however, thought that HBO could do more. He wanted the network to create its own brand of content that would attract the sophisticated viewers.

HBO began this experiment with comedy, broadcasting stand-up shows by comedians such as Robin Williams, Richard Pryor, and Billy Crystal. In 1992, the company introduced a spoof talk show called *The Larry Sanders Show*, which became wildly successful and ran for six years. In 1997, HBO moved into drama with its weekly show *Oz*, set in a fictional prison. The show astonished viewers with its frank portrayal of racial tension, homosexuality, and drugs. The content of *Oz* was far too violent and sexual for network television, but as a subscription channel HBO was not subject to the same FCC regulations.

The Sopranos, launched in 1999, once again pushed the envelope of programming. The series depicted events in the life of mobsters in New Jersey, as they went about stealing, murdering, womanizing, and handling their family responsibilities. The hero was morally bankrupt and the plots were complicated and often left unresolved, both qualities that were antithetical to the existing conventions of

INTERVIEW

The Personal Is Professional

Marcia Kavanaugh

Director of local initiatives, WYES public broadcasting, New Orleans

How did you get into television?

I became involved in student government at LSUNO, which got me interested in politics, [as] Watergate was happening. Young people my age were really tuned into opposing the Vietnam War, questioning public decisions, and I was keenly interested and getting increasingly involved. I was watching news reporting and seeing women reporting—this also coincided with the women's movement, and attempts to get more women involved in the media.

In 1971, Ed Planer, the news director of WDSU (the NBC affiliate in New Orleans) came to speak to the public opinion class taught by my faculty adviser. I had mentioned to my adviser that I was really interested in Watergate and journalism, so after the talk the adviser introduced me to Ed. He invited me to the station, and I basically created my own internship since there were no such things at the time. I just wouldn't go away. I went there more days than not. I got to log film (describe scenes or sound bits and time them), file film in the archive, run film from point A to point B, and even did a little writing. I took a journalism course in college and got to use film from the station for my final project. I did that for about a year and a half because I wanted in.

Then they hired me for the summer as a minority intern—being a woman I was considered a minority. This really put me into the ground level of production. It was much more hands-on then, no videotape or computers to generate graphics. In May 1973 the station brought me in as an associate producer in the newsroom, and I went on to produce, report, and anchor. I did not plan it—it was completely fortuitous. But I would never have gotten that job if I hadn't been around the station all the time.

What was television like when you got started?

When I got started it was the tail end of pioneer television journalism, and I worked with some of those pioneers—for example, Bill Monroe, who made *Meet the Press* a talk show staple, had been at WDSU. Bill Slatter also worked there and went up to Chicago. Ed Planer eventually went on to become vice president of NBC News. These guys were on the ground floor of broadcast journalism. WDSU was a powerhouse of broadcast journalism in the 1960s largely for civil rights coverage, and was a well-respected operation of print journalists who had made the transition to pictures.

I consider myself very fortunate that I was able to work with these people who really pioneered broadcast journalism. This market [New Orleans] is a hotbed of reporting—we have it all, crime, corruption, natural disasters—there's never a slow news day here, and it's really grown a lot of good reporters who have gone on to be national correspondents.

The work we did then was still news-gathering focused on gathering the story, not how entertaining the story was. We were still using film. That impacted news-gathering because you had deadlines, but you had to process the film (we had a film processor in house, Don Perry, and they used to call him "The Mole-Man" because the processing room was this dark dank place). You had to wait for the film to come out and then edit it with just minutes until you went on the air. The editors were such experts that they could unravel that film, hold it to the light, and cut it. When it went on the air, say you had an interview with someone who talked about, say, floodwater, and you wanted film of floodwater to come up at the same time, you ran A roll of the talking head and B roll of the picture simultaneously on the air. The director had a very tough job coordinating that live on the air. Things sometimes broke, or rolls would be too long, or the timing could be off—lots went wrong!

Videotape changed the whole game because it was instantaneous. It was supposed to mean that you could really be out on the story and get fresher coverage, but the cameras were big and heavy and the recorders were big and heavy. WDSU was the first station in New Orleans to use videotape for in-the-field news coverage, which required a two-man crew—a shooter and videotape machine controller. We used a cart to move the machine, and it actually took more time to get that stuff out of the van and to the story than it had taken with film cameras. It actually slowed us down—it was very cumbersome, and some film guys even refused to shoot it.

What about women and minorities?
When I was still an undergraduate, WDSU hired a light-skinned, African-American woman. The managers at WDSU said her hair was too straight and made her wear an Afro wig to work for months until she refused to go along with them. She moved back to Chicago to work in public television. There were a few other women, black and white, working in the early 1970s.

Lots of the stations in south Louisiana have had female news directors, but none of them do at the moment. Employment discrimination

(continued on next page)

INTERVIEW

The Personal Is Professional (continued)

became more obvious in the 1970s and companies had to get a little more equal in their hiring of women and minorities.

What differences do you see between broadcast news then and now?
Things started changing in the 1970s with consultants who emphasized happy talk, "news you can use," and that's where it is now. I

television dramas. The show was wildly popular around the world. The success of *The Sopranos* influenced programming on other channels; networks, which had previously followed strict ideas about plots, language, and characters now attempted more complex dramas with ambiguous heroes, such as *Lost*. HBO continues to introduce edgy new dramas, such as *The Wire*, *True Blood*, and *Big Love*, as well as offbeat comedies such as *Curb Your Enthusiasm* and *Flight of the Conchords*.

Satellite

Satellite opened up a whole new world of television programming. In the 1960s and 1970s, the United States and other nations placed a number of communications satellites in orbit around the earth. These satellites could be used to deliver television signals from station to station, or even from station directly to homes.

The first satellite broadcasts appeared in the early 1960s. In 1961 AT&T, Bell Labs, NASA, and the British and French post offices entered a multi-national agreement to develop two mobile telecommunications satellites. On July 10, 1962, the consortium launched the TELSTAR satellite from Kennedy Space Center in Florida. The next day, the satellite broadcast a television program from Andover, Maine, to Pleumeur-Bodou, France, the world's first transatlantic transmission of a television signal.

The success of satellite broadcasting ushered in a new era in news programming. From now on, people could learn about events in distant places almost as soon as they happened, or even watch them went back to news reporting about ten years ago after taking several years off. I remember that around that time there was this document at libraries that was a proposed master plan for the city of NO. I suggested that this was something that we really should report to help people understand what this was about. I was told that this was not "TV," i.e. that it wouldn't make a good TV news story and that we should leave it to the newspapers. Instead the person on the desk made me interview the mother of a mother-daughter pair who got in a bar fight. I said there was no way—I haven't been in this business for 30 years to do this kind of crap. But unfortunately that's the kind of thing a lot of serious news reporters have had to battle. Some newsrooms still do excellent investigative reporting, but you have to fight for it.

happening. This was crucial for reports of the Vietnam War and other events of the 1960s. For most viewers, however, the fact that their news came from a satellite was of no relevance to the way they received the news; it still had to come through a local broadcaster.

In the 1980s satellite television was fairly uncommon, restricted to viewers in remote locations who were willing to install giant satellite dishes next to their homes. In the mid-1990s, however, television companies began selling digital satellite dishes that were only 18 inches in diameter and could easily be mounted on an exterior wall. This caused an explosion in satellite television subscribers. With satellite service, viewers could now receive literally hundreds of channels.

Modern Changes

During the first decade of the 21st century, television continued to be a huge business. New technology such as plasma screen televisions, flat screen LCD televisions, HDTV, DVDs, and Blu-ray DVDs all appeared during the decade. Television networks and film studios began producing content in high-definition digital format instead of the analog format that had been used for most of television's history. The FCC decided that starting in 2009, all television broadcasts would be digital, a move that would necessarily result in anyone still using an older television with an antenna losing their television reception. To help these people, the federal government promised converters to anyone who still lacked cable or satellite television reception.

Many experts in the early 2000s believed that television was on the verge of a major transformation in business model. As of 2009, no one was exactly sure where television would go. The proliferation of channels and programs made it increasingly difficult for individual shows to capture large audiences. Viewers were using more and more technology such as DVRs and iTunes to customize the programming they watched. There was no longer any need to schedule one's day to catch programs when they aired or to sit through the many minutes of advertising interspersed throughout shows. The introduction of reality television called into question the need for scriptwriters or professional performers. Networks had more and more difficulty persuading advertisers to back new shows.

Television is still a major industry, and viewers clearly want as much programming as networks and stations can provide them. The trick for the next decade or two is to find a way to make the enterprise profitable.

A Brief Chronology

1884: Photographic film invented by George Eastman.

1887: Thomas Edison patents a camera that takes moving pictures.

1926: NBC founded as a radio network.

1928: CBS founded as a radio network.

1931: Vladimir Zworykin patents the iconoscope.

1934: FCC established.

1939: RCA's David Sarnoff introduces television at the World's Fair in New York City.

1943: Edward Noble buys NBC Blue, which becomes known as ABC.

1945: There are nine television stations and fewer than 7,000 television sets in the United States.

1946: DuMont television network founded.

1948: The FCC puts a freeze on the granting of new station licenses; hundreds of applications from around the country languish for four years.

1949: There are now 98 television stations in the United States.

1951: *I Love Lucy* debuts on CBS. CBS attempts the first color broadcast.

1952: 20 million United States households own television sets.

1955: CBS premiers two popular shows: the western *Gunsmoke*, which runs for the next 20 years, and *The $64,000 Question*, kicking off a game show craze.

1956: CBS broadcasts the film *The Wizard of Oz*. This becomes a much-anticipated annual event.

1958: Advertisers spend $2 billion on television and radio commercials.

1960: Presidential candidates, John F. Kennedy and Richard Nixon debate each other on national television, ushering in a new era of political campaigning focused more on appearances.

1963: Millions of viewers watch Martin Luther King Jr.'s "I Have a Dream" speech on August 28 and John F. Kennedy's assassination on November 22. Sports broadcasters introduce the instant replay.

1964: 73 millions viewers watch the Beatles on the *Ed Sullivan Show*.

1965: NBC begins broadcasting most of its content in color.

1969: *Sesame Street* is launched on PBS. Millions watch Neil Armstrong land on the moon. Tobacco companies agree to stop advertising cigarettes on television; this costs networks millions of dollars in advertising.

1971: The standard length of commercials drops from 60 to 30 seconds.

1972: HBO founded.

1974: ABC, CBS, and NBC share the job of covering the Watergate hearings, giving up advertising revenue for that airtime.

1976: Ted Turner founds WTBS, Atlanta, the cable "superstation."

1977: Three-quarters of American television sets can receive color broadcasts. ABC airs the miniseries *Roots*.

1979: ESPN begins broadcasts on cable.

1980: CNN and MTV begin cable broadcasts.

1983: 125 million homes tune in to the broadcast of the last episode of *M*A*S*H*.

1986: The Spanish-language channel Telemundo is launched.

1987: Rupert Murdoch launches the Fox Broadcasting Company. More than half of United States households have cable.

1988: Nearly 60 percent of United States households own a videocassette recorder.

1993: 98 percent of United States households own at least one television.

1994: 95 million viewers watch O.J. Simpson, suspected of murdering his former wife, run from police on the freeways of Los Angeles.

2000: The DVD becomes the format of choice for recorded movies. AOL and Time Warner merge.

2003: The first DVD camcorder is released.

2005: Most televisions sold have plasma or flat LCD screens.

2006: Blu-Ray DVDs appear.

2009: All television networks switch to high definition digital broadcasts.

Chapter 2

State of the Industry

The U.S. Department of Labor divides up the different aspects of the television industry into several of its industry classifications, including broadcasting and motion picture and video production. The department puts television, video, and motion picture camera operators and editors in their own category. There is considerable overlap within these categories.

Broadcast television is considered part of the broadcasting industry, along with radio. Within the broadcasting industry, 66 percent of workers are employed either in television broadcasting or cable broadcasting. The rest work in radio. The U.S. Department of Labor technically considers cable and pay television distributors to be part of the telecommunications industry, not the broadcast industry, but many of the jobs are the same. The motion picture and video industry produces films for the wide screen and television.

The broadcast industry consists of stations and networks that broadcast live and pre-recorded programs to viewers. These programs travel over the airwaves, satellite distribution systems, or cable television lines to the television sets of viewers. Television networks and stations broadcast a wide variety of programs, including news, dramas, sitcoms, talk shows, sports programs, movies, and other types of entertainment. Individual networks and stations produce some of their own content, particularly local news programs and talk shows, and purchase the rest. Many television networks own production companies that produce content, such as television series and movies.

The United States motion picture and video industry produces feature films and recorded television programs, made-for television movies, music videos and commercials, but does not broadcast those programs. This industry is dominated by several large studios based in Hollywood; the remainder are small- and medium-sized production companies that either produce films and programs themselves or work as contractors providing postproduction services to the big studios. Many of these companies are owned by television networks, which use them to produce content.

Funding

Commercial television stations and networks get their funding from the sale of advertising time. Advertising is a very big business. Networks and individual stations set rates for advertising by time of day, likely size of audience for a given program, and demographic characteristics such as age, sex, and median family income. Programs with huge audiences of desirable demographics, such as the Super Bowl-can sell extremely expensive advertising time. In 2009, for example, a 30-second Super Bowl ad cost $3 million dollars. It was estimated to have reached about 9 million viewers, many of them young and middle-aged men who tend to be big spenders.

Cable and satellite television stations and networks earn their revenue from a combination of subscriber fees and advertising. Educational stations and other noncommercial stations rely on grants and donations from the government, individuals, and corporations. These stations are not operated for profit. Public broadcasting stations purchase content and occasionally still produce their own programs.

Statistics on Employment, Wages, and Profits

As of 2006 about 130,000 people worked in television broadcasting and around 90,000 worked in cable broadcasting. About three quarters of these jobs were in establishments with at least 50 employees, most of these concentrated in large cities. Smaller stations are spread throughout the country. At small television stations, employees often find themselves performing several jobs instead of specializing in one area. This makes small stations a great place for new television employees to gain experience in the field.

The following are the Bureau of Labor Statistics 2006 figures for people working in broadcasting in 2006. These statistics include only those who work in broadcast television, not cable, and they also include some people who work primarily in radio:

Radio and television announcers 38,000

Actors, producers, and directors 26,000

Reporters and correspondents 10,000

Computer specialists 9,000

Editors 4,000

Film and video editors 4,000

Engineers 3,000

Writers and authors 3,000

Graphic designers 2,000

Multi-media artists and animators 1,000

In all, some 148,000 people were working for wages or salaries in professional and related occupations within the motion picture and video industries; some of these people worked exclusively in television or motion pictures, and some did both. Another 20,000 or so worked on the management and financial side of film and video production. Competition for these jobs is very keen. Employment of television announcers is declining as stations consolidate.

About 71,000 people were working as television and radio announcers in 2006. About half of them were actually employed by networks; the rest worked part time or as self-employed freelancers. The self-employed often sell their services to a number of different clients, including networks and stations, advertising agencies, or sponsors of local events.

The BLS reported that about 163,000 people were working as actors, producers, and directors in all media, including television, film, video, and on stage. There is a fair amount of movement between these media; it is common for an actor or producer to work in both television and film, and to spend some time working with live theater as well. Competition for jobs is extremely high, and actors, producers, and directors all spend a fair amount of time unemployed. The numbers of people working for wages or salary within the motion picture and video industries in 2006 are as follows:

Entertainers and performers 44,000

Actors 19,000

Producers and directors 18,000

Film and video editors 11,000

Camera operators 9,000

Multimedia artists and animators 7,000

Computer specialists 5,000

Editors 4,000

Graphic designers 3,000

Writers and authors 2,000

In 2006, about 27,000 people were working as television, video, and motion picture camera operators; another 21,000 were employed as film and video editors. Most of these individuals worked in large metropolitan areas such as New York City or Los Angeles. About 17 percent of these workers were self-employed. Of the salaried workers, about half worked for television studios and half for motion picture studios, some of which were producing movies for television. Independent television stations, small independent production companies, large cable and television networks, and local affiliate stations of broadcast groups or television networks also provided a large number of jobs.

Hours and Working Conditions

Television programs are broadcast 24 hours a day, and that means that employees are working around the clock to ensure that content appears at the right time. Erratic work hours are the norm. You may find yourself working early mornings, late nights, or weekends. On the other hand, although many television professionals also work very long hours, the average workweek for broadcasting employees in 2006 was 36 hours. Those erratic hours can also translate into a flexible schedule, which many people consider highly desirable. Part-time work is the exception in broadcasting; in 2006, only 9 percent of broadcast employees worked part-time.

Film and video production has even more erratic hours than broadcasting. Part-time work is more common in that part of the television industry; in 2006, 42 percent of workers had either part-time or variable schedules, and the average workweek was 29 hours. Many people who work in television production are freelance. This is particularly true of actors and writers, and these workers may not be able to support themselves entirely on their earnings from television work. Intermittent employment and regular rejection are the rule rather than the exception for many people who work on the production side.

Work environment varies by position. Some people spend all their time indoors, in offices or studios. These are typically clean, well-lit, and comfortable, though if you work in a studio you must be aware of the presence of cables and camera equipment. Other television workers spend their days (or nights!) driving around or working in the field. Reporters who shoot stories on location must work in the places where their stories are happening. This can be uncomfortable or even downright dangerous. Have you ever seen a weather reporter standing out in a hurricane in a raincoat? Remember that there are also cameraman and other technicians out there. Field service engineers may have to repair transmission equipment on poles or towers in bad weather. News reporters and technicians who work in war zones must contend with explosions, bullet fire, and other hazards.

Jobs within the television industry can be quite stressful. People who work in broadcast journalism must constantly meet deadlines, sometimes with only minutes or seconds to spare. Videotape (VT) operators and directors may have to find and broadcast clips on the fly; this is particularly true for anyone who works with live broadcasts, especially sporting events.

Directors and producers are under constant pressure to meet deadlines and stay within budgets, all while managing large groups of people. Actors, writers, and other creative workers face regular criticism of themselves and their work and must often redo the same thing (shooting a scene, writing a script) repeatedly until the producer or director is satisfied.

Salary and Wages

The average weekly earnings of workers in broadcasting in 2006 was $827. The highest pay was in large metropolitan areas. The median weekly earnings for wage and salary workers in film and video production $593 in 2006. This number conceals the fact that pay actually varies widely within the industry.

Actors who belong to the Screen Actors Guild must be paid a minimum daily rate of $759, or $2,634 for a five-day week. Actors receive extra payment when networks and stations run reruns of shows in which they appear. Before you get the impression that working as an actor is the road to riches, remember that many actors work intermittently, sometimes only a few days at a time. Most actors supplement their earnings with other jobs; working in the restaurant industry is common because hours can be flexible enough to allow actors to take time off when they have acting gigs. Successful actors may earn very high salaries, but even they may have trouble maintaining consistent employment. Salaries for directors of television films and programs vary widely. Producers may earn a percentage of a show's earnings rather than receiving a salary.

Median hourly earnings of occupations, May 2006:

General and operations managers $44.65

Producers and directors $34.01

Camera operators $21.16

Reporters and correspondents $18.27

Audio and video equipment technicians $16.60

Entertainers and performers $15.58

Radio and television announcers $11.55

Actors $10.69

Larger television stations and networks offer their salaried employees a full range of benefits, including health insurance, retirement plans, and paid vacation and sick leave. Smaller employers may not be able to offer the same benefits. Freelancers do not receive benefits at all and must procure their own health insurance and retirement coverage.

The Importance of Timing

The time of day and day of the week is very significant to television networks. Different people watch television at different times. Early in the morning adults may watch television for a little while as they prepare themselves for work; they want shows that give them quick information in a user-friendly fashion and that they can abandon at any point. During the morning and early afternoon, the main viewers are children under the age of five, women who stay at home, and retirees. The kids want cartoons and shows with fun characters, while their parents want education, so this is the main time slot for educational children's programming. The adults want entertainment and gossip; soap operas and talk shows are popular fare for this audience.

Later in the day, older kids come home. Networks broadcast teen and preteen dramas and cartoons for them. Traditionally local news stations have broadcast their news programs at 5 P.M. and 6 P.M., to reach the audience of workers who have just gotten home. Prime time, from 7 P.M. or 8 P.M. until 10 P.M. or 11 P.M., is the timeslot with the largest and most diverse audiences; families have eaten dinner, everyone is tired, and families of all descriptions are likely to sit down together to watch television. Advertisers pay top dollar for these timeslots and networks reserve their most popular programs, which may be comedies, dramas, reality shows, sporting events, or movies. After prime time, the children are in bed. Networks can now use profanity, and late-night talk show hosts may bring on controversial guests. Some people do watch television all night long, but networks and advertisers rarely bother to lavish much attention on the midnight to 6 A.M. timeslot, instead filling it with reruns, old movies, home shopping, and other inexpensive content.

Types of Television Programs

Over the years, the variety of television programs has grown exponentially. One can now find shows—and, in many cases, entire channels—catering to virtually every niche market imaginable.

Broadcast Journalism

Broadcast journalism, or broadcast news, is news broadcast on television, radio, or the Internet, as opposed to print journalism, which is printed on newspapers or in magazines. Broadcast journalism is one of the areas where there is still a need for locally produced television content. People who work in this area often work in smaller local stations, pursuing their own stories and putting them together from the ground up. Broadcast news stations need all types of technical workers, reporters, anchors and other newscasters, directors, news writers, and many other employees. At smaller stations, employees may find themselves doing a variety of different jobs.

Documentaries

Documentary films are films that depict and describe true events. Documentaries use film footage, interviews, narration, graphics, and other devices to educate viewers about their topics. Documentaries are supposed to be nonfiction; documentary makers attempt to capture their subjects without staging events or coaching their subjects in what to say. Documentary production is quite similar to news reporting, and many broadcast news stations often produce longer documentaries to supplement their news coverage. Working on a documentary may require weeks of carrying cameras and sound equipment to various locations, finding interview subjects, researching, and then editing hours of footage to tell a story in a smooth and objective way.

Dramas

Dramas are shows that tell stories that are not explicitly comedies. Dramas include police programs, hospital shows, crime shows, shows set in courthouses, and shows that portray events in family lives. Dramatic series usually have a stable cast of characters who appear in every episode and story lines that may be completed in single episodes or run through an entire season of shows. Dramatic shows have a great deal in common with films, and the professionals who work on them often work in film as well. Dramas provide great opportunities for most television professionals, including actors, technicians and artists, and especially writers, who must produce tight scripts on a regular basis. Many writers break into television by writing spec scripts for dramas. The shows often use elaborate sets, carefully written scripts, and top-notch professionals. Television professionals who like working on high-quality productions love working on dramas. Dramas are expensive to produce, though, which is why many networks are backing off on producing them, often in favor of unscripted reality shows.

Game Shows

A game show is a television program in which participants play a game in order to win prizes. Participants are often non-performers who may be picked out of a studio audience or go through a process of application. Sometimes celebrities participate. The games may require a high level of skill or specialized knowledge for success, and most of them reward contestants who can think well on their feet. *Jeopardy* features people answering questions on various topics. *The Price is Right* tests contestants' knowledge of the prices of consumer goods such as cleaning supplies, packaged foods, or appliances. Today game shows may have an audience participation component, such as the "Ask the Audience" lifeline on *Who Wants to Be a Millionaire*. Most game shows, like talk shows, are filmed in a studio with a minimal cast and crew. They may involve a great deal of work communicating with advertisers and would-be contestants.

Reality Television

Reality television is a television genre that broadcasts live, unscripted situations, typically edited to heighten drama or comedy. Reality television shows may use hidden cameras to capture completely natural footage of people reacting to surprising situations, a technique that was employed on the show *Candid Camera*. Today, reality television usually involves performers who are perfectly aware that they are being filmed going about their daily business but possibly in alien surroundings. Participants may try to improve themselves or find a spouse. They may participate in a contest in which participants are eliminated one by one. A participant may simply try to inhabit a new environment with new companions, such as in the show *Big Brother*.

Television writers sometimes disparage reality television because it does not require their services, at least not in the traditional way; reality shows do use writers to outline action before or after filming, but this role is minor compared to writing complete scripts. The shows are often essentially unscripted, which gave them a commercial advantage during the television writers' strike of 2007–2008. Reality television does employ a number of other workers, though; makeup artists, camera operators, directors, producers, and many others can all find jobs in reality television.

Situation Comedies

A situation comedy, or sitcom, is a television comedy that involves a steady cast of characters and a stable setting; in other words, the characters are in essentially the same situation in every episode. Sitcoms have scripts, and actors are not expected to improvise.

Problem Solving

Camera operators need to by physically fit and strong enough to lift and carry relatively heavy equipment. "Jonathan" learned this through experience. He was hired to spend a month in Venice, Italy, shooting footage of a project that a team of scholars was working on in the Biblioteca Marciana. It sounded like a dream job, and in many ways it was. It was also very hard, physical work. Jonathan kept his equipment in his apartment, about a mile away from the library. Every morning he had to carry his camera, camera stand, reflectors, and microphone to the library to film the work. Many days he also had to carry all that equipment to other locations within Venice to shoot interviews with project team members. Twice he did interviews in gondolas floating through the city's canals—getting into a boat with a heavy camera and then hooking up a microphone to an interview subject is quite a challenge! Jonathan was young and strong, so he did fine with the physical side of the job, but the experience certainly left him with a much greater appreciation for the joys of stationary studio work.

Characters are clearly and simply drawn so that viewers know what to expect from them, and the same jokes often appear in multiple episodes. Character and plot development are kept to a minimum so that the overall situation remains the same, though many sitcoms do have plots that develop over the course of a season or even over many years. Sitcoms employ all types of television workers. A successful sitcom can provide a television professional with years of work, though many sitcoms last only a short time, falling victim to low ratings and the whims of networks.

Soap Operas

A soap opera, or soap, is a dramatic television series in which a story is told in serial form. Each episode leads up to the next episode, creating a continuous story. Often an episode will end with a cliffhanger to capture viewers for the next episode. Many daytime soaps broadcast a new episode every weekday. Primetime soap operas may broadcast weekly. Soap operas have been popular since before the days of television, when radio stations would broadcast continuing stories; the name "soap opera" came from the sponsors, who were often soap manufacturers advertising to their largely female audience. Daytime soaps today are still aimed at female viewers, housewives, and stay-at-home moms. Their plots tend to be romantic and occasionally melodramatic with a large cast of characters. Soap operas employ large numbers of actors and crew people; working on a soap can be stressful because episodes must be shot very quickly. In fact, in the early days of television, soap operas were broadcast live.

Sports Events

People throughout the world watch sports on television. Sports broadcasts include coverage of actual events plus a great deal of extra information, such as interviews with players and coaches, human interest stories about athletes, information on teams or sports history, and other content that might be of interest to viewers. Broadcasting sporting events requires large crews of technical people, especially skilled camera operators and editors who can cut from shot to shot on the fly. Sportscasters tend to be very knowledgeable about the sports they cover. They are often former athletes or coaches in the sports that they cover, so if you have a background as a college or professional athlete or maybe some Olympic experience, this could be a good field for you.

Talk Shows

A talk show is a television program in which a host invites guests to appear on the show to talk to him or her. Talk shows are wildly popular, especially on daytime television and late at night. Guests may be celebrities such as movie stars, television actors, musicians, or authors. They may also be regular people who have done extraordinary things or who have unusual problems. Some talk show hosts are known for showing empathy to their guests. Other are famous for mixing guests who have reason to hate one another and who often get into fights on camera. *The Oprah Winfrey Show* is one of the most popular long-running talk shows on television. Talk shows are usually shot in a single studio with a fairly minimal staff, but a talk show job can be good steady work for a television professional.

Television Commercials and Infomercials

Television commercials are short programs produced that are shown during breaks in television programs in an effort to sell products. The companies that want to sell the products pay for the production and broadcasting of commercials. They may pay an advertising agency to produce the commercial, and then pay the television network or station for airtime. An infomercial is a longer commercial, at least five minutes long, that purports to educate customers about a product while attempting to persuade them to buy it. (Some infomercials are much longer than five minutes, stretching to 30 minutes or an hour; these usually air during the dead zone of midnight to 6 A.M.) Thousands of commercials appear on television every day, and advertisers constantly want new ones, making this field a rich one for those aspiring to careers in television.

Current Trends

There are television jobs throughout the United States. Although most jobs are concentrated in big cities, especially in Los Angeles and New York, there are still local stations in most midsize cities. Many television professionals, particularly those who work in broadcast news, start out at small local stations and then work their way up to bigger venues. Smaller stations may offer easier entry and greater initial responsibility, but larger stations have more jobs available and more room to move up. The consolidation of television networks has resulted in fewer independent local jobs than existed late in the 20th century. At the moment, work in traditional dramatic and comedy shows is getting harder to find, while reality shows are getting more popular. There is an increasing need for professionals who can work with digital media and computer animation.

Competition for jobs in television is fierce, especially in large cities. Many people think a job in television would be glamorous. Many of those already working in the industry do find their jobs exciting and rewarding, though they may no longer worry about glamour. The jobs with the most competition are the most visible and often the highest paying: jobs in acting, writing, producing, and directing are all very difficult to get. More technical behind-the-scenes jobs such as editing are less glutted.

Because competition is so keen, broadcasters have no need to provide on-the job training to workers. There is usually an oversupply of qualified applicants for any job, so employers need hire only those who can do any given job immediately. Most jobs go to applicants who have college degrees in journalism, broadcasting, communications studies, or a similar field, and who have experience working in college television stations. Internships and page programs are another source of experience that can lead to a job. NBC, for example, has a famous page program that has introduced many newcomers to television careers. This program, like many internship programs in the field, is extremely competitive and difficult to enter.

That being said, there are some entry-level positions that are historically given to applicants with little experience in the field, though a degree in broadcasting is a huge help. Production assistants do not need much experience. The same goes for writers' assistants and other types of assistants. The trade-off, of course, is that these positions usually pay very little. Job seekers take them, however, because they are a great way of entering the industry. Working as a production assistant allows people to learn the industry from the bottom up and to make the connections that are so crucial to succeeding in this field. If you work as a PA on one show, chances are you will be able to call your supervisor to help you when you want another better job later on.

Once you have landed a position in television, your training will be less important than your talent, creativity, experience, professionalism, and connections. If you are already working in the television industry, cultivating good relationships is one of the best ways to help your career advance.

Many entry-level television jobs are at smaller stations. It is not unusual for a person who wants to work in television to spend several years moving around from place to place, working his or her way up from an entry-level job in a small city to a mid-range job in a larger metropolitan area.

As of 2009, reality television was one of the big trends of the decade. Networks rejoiced to discover that not only were reality shows much cheaper to produce than scripted programs, they were also wildly popular. Audiences love them. Unfortunately for television workers, reality shows use fewer professionals than other types of programming.

Television in general was trying to get by with fewer writers. The Television Writers Strike of 2007–2008 convinced many network executives that writers were not always necessary. Writers who worked on reality shows, though, spent a great deal of effort convincing networks that they played a vital role in creating the finished product and working to get paid for their contributions.

Viewers are getting increasingly skilled at customizing their programming and avoiding advertisements. Advertisers are looking for new ways to reach customers. They are experimenting with techniques such as interactive television advertisements, advertisements placed in menus, advertisements placed in video-on-demand programming, and advertisements in the online streams of television shows.

Possible Future Trends

The Department of Labor expects employment in the television industry to grow about 11 percent between 2006 and 2016, which is about average for all industries in the United States. Job growth will be the result of an increasing demand for programming as the number of cable and satellite television channels explodes in the United States and abroad. Demand for Internet films, videos, and DVDs to be shown in homes should increase steadily. Audiences will become increasingly fragmented, resulting in many more opportunities to create unique content for specialty networks. More and more foreign countries will become able to watch television, which will increase demand for programming, especially television dramas and movies. The reason job growth will not be higher is that turnover will be high; a number of workers will leave their jobs in television to take jobs in more stable industries with less stress and more regular hours.

There will be an increased need for workers skilled in digital filming, computer editing and animation, computer-generated imaging, general film and video editing, and multimedia artists and animators. There will also be more need for workers skilled in broadcast and sound technology, gaffers, set builders, and other technical jobs.

Those seeking more glamorous jobs, particularly actors, writers, producers, and directors, will face ever fiercer competition for those positions. Growth in those areas is not expected to grow especially fast, and more and more people are expected to seek those jobs.

Outsourcing of television production is becoming concern for television producers. United States film and video producers have started filming productions in other countries with lower costs. This is especially true for low-budget films, which include many made-for-television movies and commercials. English-speaking countries, particularly Canada, offer tax breaks to filmmakers who bring film productions to them. Television and film workers who live in the United States dislike this trend because it takes away jobs; production companies typically hire many local people to work as production assistants, drivers, technicians, and for minor acting roles. Several American cities and states offer tax breaks to film production companies who film their programs in their localities.

Advertising will become less and less effective as viewers use technology to avoid television commercials. Many marketers have observed the declining effectiveness of their television advertisements over the past few years and looked ahead to the day when they must stop investing so much in television advertising. A 2008 survey by the Association of National Advertisers found that a majority of marketers expect to cut their television advertising expenditures when 50 percent of United States households use DVRs; At the time of the study coverage was about 23 percent, so this will likely happen in just a few years. Marketers are considering shifting their advertising budgets to the Internet.

New Media

New media refers to digital and computerized communications, such as the Internet. The term *new media* is used to contrast these forms with older media such as radio, television, and print.

The television industry is encountering increasing competition from new media. The more time people spend surfing the Internet, texting, or similarly engaged, the less time they spend watching television. The Internet offers its own supply of video content, too, which keeps people away from their television sets.

Television networks today are working hard to integrate their programming into a world that includes new media. Web sites, blogs, online trailers, and chat rooms devoted to particular television shows attract viewers who are not satisfied with just watching their favorite programs and who want to enhance their experience by communicating with fellow fans online, or who want to watch shows on their own schedules, not restricted to some networks time slots.

New media can also revolutionize television production. The BBC, for example, has envisioned a fully digital production process

Professional Ethics

2007–2008 Writers Guild of America Strike

In November 2007, the members of the Writers Guild of America, East and Writers Guild of America, West went on strike. Their complaint–the typical complaint of any strike–was that they were not being paid enough money for the work they did.

The Alliance of Motion Picture and Television Production (AMPTP) and Writers Guild of America (WGA) set the terms of writers' compensation in a contract that is re-negotiated every three years. The writers were concerned that they would not be adequately compensated for residuals for so-called new media, which includes Internet downloads, streaming, straight-to-Internet content, video on demand, and electronic sell-through (such as sales through the iTunes store). When the AMPTP refused to budge, the writers stopped working.

For 100 days writers picketed and refused to produce scripts for television programs. Production of shows came to a standstill. Desperate studios scrambled to fill the airwaves with new programming, with mixed success. Reality shows were a popular choice. The strike ended on February 12, 2008, when almost 94 percent of WGA members voted to ratify an agreement with the AMPTP providing a higher pay rate for writers.

Was the writers' strike ethical? Many people, particularly television professionals who lost jobs while the strike went on, thought it was not. The writers knew when they began their strike that their actions would affect other people. Studios and literary agencies laid off workers. Networks lost viewers, and advertisers withdrew their funding as ratings dropped. Various experts estimated that the strike cost the economy of Los Angeles between $380 million and $2.1 billion. And what about the profit margin of the new media? You will have to keep watching to see how that turns out.

that will create open, accessible, and interoperable networks. This will make it possible for teams in different places to access and share content and to produce integrated programming that will do a better job of communicating stories than television alone.

Is Television a Dying Industry?

If you start talking to people who work in television, chances are that one of them will refer to the field as a "dying industry." It is true that much has changed in television in recent years. The proliferation of cable and satellite channels that occurred in the 1980s and 1990s greatly increased competition for viewers. The consolidation of media companies has resulted in many fewer local stations than there were late in the twentieth century. Reality television has been wildly successful, leading some to conclude that writers and professional performers are largely unnecessary. The writers' strike of 2007–2008 went even further to convince networks that it did not need writers to produce popular content. Certainly reality shows are cheaper for networks to produce than scripted programs; depending on the show, the network may save a great deal by not having to pay actors, writers, set designers, makeup artists, and all the other professionals involved in dramas. One major source of savings is not having to pay union rates to performers. Reality shows may also avoid having to pay residuals to writers.

The business model that kept network television running during the second half of the twentieth century no longer works as it once did. As of 2009, advertisers were cautious about buying ad time during programs. New media and DVRs have made it less likely that viewers will actually see their commercials, and advertising slots are expensive. Attendees at that year's May upfront in New York were filled with uncertainty about the economy, about the likelihood that the highly touted new shows would go the distance and not be cancelled during their first seasons (even after their first episodes), and about the effectiveness of advertising on television.

What is the truth? There seems to be no shortage of programs on television and hits still appear regularly. The average American watched 151 hours of television in 2008. Television advertising is still fairly effective, at least compared to the alternatives such as print or online advertising, though a majority of television advertisers in 2008 said that television advertising had become less effective over the previous two years. Many industry professionals maintain that there are still television jobs available. The fact is that television has always been a highly competitive and unpredictable field. There is still tremendous demand for video entertainment, in whatever form the business takes.

Important Technology

Television is a continuously developing medium. What follows are some of the most significant advances of recent times.

Closed Captioning

Closed captioning is a method of displaying a transcript of a television program's audio track on the bottom of the screen, similar to subtitles on a foreign film. This transcript makes it possible for hearing-impaired people to get the same content from a program as hearing viewers. The closed captions do not appear on every broadcast, even when they are available; a viewer must use a decoder to make them visible on the screen.

The quality of captions varies depending on the method used to produce them. Captions transcribed before a broadcast can be quite accurate, but for live broadcasts, the captions are prepared on the fly. For live broadcasts, a human being repeats all sounds into a stenomask, a device used to record speech verbatim. A computer takes this content and converts it into text. This method produces fairly accurate captions, but sometimes the captions fall behind the action and occasionally the computer produces words that are not exactly right.

Digital Television

Digital television (DTV) is television that is broadcast through digital signals, unlike earlier television broadcasts, which used analog signals. In the United States, broadcasters stopped transmitting analog signals on June 12, 2009. From that day forward, all television signals were digital. This was a potentially controversial transition because it required all viewers to have either a television capable of receiving digital signals or to acquire a converter box. In practice, it did not appear to generate much difficulty. Other countries around the world have set their own dates for converting to digital broadcasts.

HDTV

HDTV, or high definition television, is high-definition digital television broadcasting. The image quality of HDTV broadcasts is higher than that of traditional broadcasts. HDTV has been around since 1998. By 2009, most televisions sold in the United States were HDTVs. High definition television displays can use LCDs, plasma, or rear-projection systems to create images. The full benefit of HDTV only occurs when a viewer has a high definition television and the broadcast he or she is watching is also in high definition. Television networks are in the process of converting all their broadcasts to high definition, a process that will accelerate now that all television signals are digital. Until that happens, many broadcasts will still appear in standard definition.

Video on Demand

Video on Demand, or VOD, is technology that allows viewers to choose their own television content, thereby escaping the scheduling and advertising imposed by networks. This practice is known as "timeshifting." Viewers use electronics to download content from the Internet and view it on various devices, including phones, computers, and television sets.

Major Players and Industry Forces

Below are the most influential forces in shaping the future of television.

Broadcast Networks

In the United States, television broadcasting comes through networks. Local station affiliates broadcast network content to their local markets, and usually supplement network content with their own locally produced programming. The main broadcast networks include:

Best Practice

Television networks sell advertising for their new seasons at events called "upfronts," which are conferences attended by television network executives and major advertising companies. The press also attends in force. The United States networks hold their upfronts in New York every May. At an upfront, the networks screen samples of their new programs in an attempt to convince advertisers that the shows will be hits and thus worthy of heavy investments in advertising. The advertisers choose the shows they like and purchase ad time "up front," before the shows begin airing.

➜ NBC: National Broadcasting Company, with its headquarters in Rockefeller Center in New York City. (The NBC comedy *30 Rock* took its name from NBC Studios' street address.) Its logo is a peacock.

➡ ABC: American Broadcasting Company, owned by the Walt Disney Company. It has offices in New York City and Burbank, California.

➡ CBS: formerly known as the Columbia Broadcasting System. Its logo is a stylized black and white eye.

➡ FOX: Fox Broadcasting Company, a relative newcomer to the broadcast television networks. It was founded in 1986 and gradually built its market share to become one of the most popular stations by the mid-2000s. In 1996, FOX introduced Fox News Channel, which gradually captured the largest share of viewers of television news programs. FOX launched a new network, myNetworkTV, in 2006.

➡ The CW: a new network launched in 2006 as a joint venture between CBS and Warner Brothers. It arose after the demise of two other short-lived networks, UPN and the WB television network.

➡ PBS: Public Broadcasting System, the American nonprofit public television network. It is funded by the Corporation for Public Broadcasting and has its headquarters in Arlington, Virginia, and Burbank, California. Its logo is a black circle with stylized human profiles stacked within it.

Cable and Satellite Networks

Cable and satellite networks use a different broadcasting model from the broadcast networks. Because their content comes through cables or is sent from satellites, they do not need affiliate stations in local networks, though they do sometimes use form alliances with local stations. Networks also form alliances with each other and with other networks and corporations, especially motion picture production companies. Aside from differences in broadcasting methods, the distinction between cable and satellite networks and broadcast networks is that viewers pay to watch cable and satellite channels but can receive broadcast channels for free. Some cable stations also accept fees from advertisers and run commercials during their programs. Other networks are technically known as premium television services because they do not broadcast commercials during their programming.

Hundreds of cable and satellite networks are now available to viewers. These range from giant operations such as CNN and HBO

On the Cutting Edge

Television companies and electronics manufacturers have been frantically trying to introduce new technology that will captivate viewers while keeping up with rapid developments in new media. Consumers, on the other hand, are most interested in controlling what they watch and watching it when they want to—preferably without any advertisements.

On the consumer's side are technology such as digital video recorders (DVRs), Apple TV, streaming, and video on demand (VOD). In a VOD system, consumers download content or have it stream through a device such as a home computer. They can then watch their programs at their leisure, skipping over any advertisements along the way. DVRs allow viewers to record programs and watch them later. Viewers who own Apple TV systems can customize their home video libraries and choose all their own viewing content. Many viewers now purchase episodes of their television programs from the iTunes music store, watching them at their convenience.

The problem with these techniques is that these viewers may avoid seeing the advertisements that were shown with the original broadcast. To encourage viewers to tune in at the same time as the rest of their peers, FOX News and CNN have both used social networking Web sites such as Twitter and Facebook to allow viewers to send questions directly to hosts on the air. The appeal of interacting with hosts may outweigh the appeal of watching the show at the most convenient time. Networks are experimenting with ways of broadcasting live over the Internet. They are also considering offering archives of old broadcasts for viewers. At the moment, however, it seems that the viewers are winning the game of avoiding advertising, leaving the television industry wondering how it will manage to change to keep up.

to small niche players such as the Gospel Music Channel. There are a number of Spanish-language channels such as Telemundo available in the United States and Canada. Cable and satellite stations are occasionally known for more daring or interesting programming because they are not held to the same standards of profanity and indecency as the broadcast networks. Some of the more prominent cable and satellite networks include:

➜ CNN: Cable News Network, the first network to offer 24 hours a day of nothing but news. It is headquartered in Atlanta, Georgia, New York City, and has studios in Los Angeles and Washington, D.C. It is owned by Time Warner.

➜ C-SPAN: Cable-Satellite Public Affairs Network, a cable television network that broadcasts live government proceedings, press conferences, House and Senate debates, and similar items. It does not broadcast advertising.

➜ Fox News: FNC, or Fox News Channel, a news channel created in 1996 by Rupert Murdoch and owned by Fox Entertainment Group. Its headquarters are in New York City.

➜ ESPN: Entertainment Sports Programming Network, a cable network that broadcasts sporting events and sports-related programming 24 hours a day. ESPN's main office is in Bristol, Connecticut.

➜ HBO: Home Box Office, owned by Time Warner. HBO broadcasts movies and original programming.

➜ Disney Channel: this cable channel broadcasts movies and programs generally aimed at younger children. It is owned by the Walt Disney Company.

➜ Nickelodeon: a cable television network that broadcasts content aimed at children of elementary and middle school age. It is owned by MTV Networks, a division of Viacom.

➜ MTV: Music Television, a cable network founded in 1981 to broadcast music videos. Since the 1990s, it has concentrated more on non-musical programming.

➜ Univision: the largest Spanish-language television network in the United States. It is headquartered in New York with offices in Miami, Florida. It broadcasts news, dramatic programming, and telenovelas produced by Mexican television corporation Grupo Televisa.

Unions

Unions dominate the television and film production industry. Anyone who wants steady work in the field must join the appropriate union or unions. In broadcasting, union membership is not as

Everyone Knows

Nielsen Ratings

In the television business, ratings are king. Every network wants to capture as many viewers as it can and every advertiser wants to know exactly how many people are seeing its commercials. This research is primarily done by Nielsen Media Research (NMR), a company that since 1950 has measured which programs people watch. It collects this data by collecting data from television sets in selected homes and by having certain audience members keep diaries of their television watching. The company tries to collect data from a variety of demographics and locations so that it can compile an accurate picture of television watching habits across the country. The ratings include information on age, sex, and economic class of viewers, all of interest to advertisers.

important; only about 8 percent of workers in broadcasting belong to unions.

Actors who work in film (including commercials, television programming, and all types of movies) belong to the Screen Actors Guild (SAG). Actors who work in broadcast television belong to the American Federation of Television and Radio Artists (AFTRA). Actors from either union may take jobs in freelance television commercial work, industrial or educational films not for broadcast, and interactive media (such as computer games). Many actors belong to both unions.

Film and television directors typically belong to the Directors Guild of America. People who work behind the scenes belong to either the United Scenic Artists Association or the International Alliance of Theatrical Stage Employees, Moving Picture Technicians, Artists and Allied Crafts (I.A.T.S.E.). These behind-the-scenes workers can include set designers, camera operators, sound technicians, art directors, editors, costumers, makeup artists, and many others.

Writers belong to Writers Guild of America. The Writers Guild of America, East (WGAE), represents television and film writers on the east coast, especially around New York City. The Writers Guild of

INTERVIEW

Seizing the opportunities

Stephen Bailey
Media specialist, Center for Visualization, University of Kentucky

How long have you worked in television? What jobs have you had?
I have worked in television for 11 years. My first job was assistant editor for *Workplace Essential Skills, a* PBS series produced through the facilities of Kentucky Educational Television (KET). Then I worked as Editor for *GED Connection* a PBS series produced through the facilities of Kentucky Educational Television (KET). After that I became a videographer/editor at Franciscan University of Steubenville. Today I work as a media specialist for the Center for Visualization at the University of Kentucky.

How did you get into the field?
It all started with a campus visit while I was still in high school. One of the tour stops was the communication art's building and I could not get enough. I have always loved to tell stories and media communications seemed like a great fit.

During college I took advantage of every opportunity to get real world experience. Through school classes I was able to run camera for several local concerts and sporting events. My junior year I was able to get some freelance jobs working for horse events and auto races. I worked as a runner (answering phones and driving talent around) for the Indianapolis 500. I also got to work on the production team for a JumboTron at the Goodwill Games in New York City.

During my senior year I got an internship at KET. My duties for the internship included driving people to and from the airport, carrying equipment, and digitizing video at night. I asked permission from the editor to cut together some of the footage that I was digitizing. I stayed late and tried to edit as much as I could. I learned the editing system and impressed the editor. They hired me to be the assistant editor as soon as I graduated.

America, West (WGAW), represents television and film writers on the west coast, in Hollywood and southern California. Both branches of the WGA belong to the International Affiliation of Writers Guilds,

What do you do now? What is your typical day like?

Currently I lead a team of media interns who produce documentary videos promoting the research at University of Kentucky. I also produce the marquee projects that come through the center. I travel around to document the research and tell the story through video.

My typical day includes a good deal of e-mail and phone calls. I need to schedule days for shooting. I organize the stories and decide how to best tell the story. Once the story is set I start scheduling the shooting schedule. Once shooting begins, I set up interviews and get all the footage necessary. Editing is where the story takes shape and starts to make sense.

How do you decide what programs to make and where to distribute them?

We look at all the research projects and find the interesting ones. We then see if the people involved in the research are interested in helping to make the video. Once they sign on we start the process. We look to different outlets to distribute depending on the content and who would be most interested.

What sort of opportunities are there in the television field?

Opportunities are everywhere for people in the television field. Traditional television stations may be cutting back and hiring [fewer] people, but there are many alternatives to the traditional stations. Cable stations are everywhere and they all need original content. In addition to the traditional and cable stations, the Internet is growing every day. With increased bandwidth and the diffusion of high-speed connections in people's homes the Internet is flooded with video content. Every Web site seems to want to include video. The opportunities are abundant.

What tips would you give to someone contemplating a career in television?

The best advice I can give is to work hard in school and take every opportunity to gain experiences that help you fit into the industry. Once you start working real jobs you will know if you are a good fit. Schooling only teaches so much. Getting out there and seeing what the field is like is invaluable. Many times opportunities are only there if you are willing to work on your own time and learn the technology. If you love television and love telling stories this might be a good field for you.

an international trade union. All of these unions work to protect the interests of writers, especially the enforcement of copyrights and the payment of royalties and residuals.

The Alliance of Motion Picture and Television Producers (AMPTP) represents nearly 400 studios and film production companies in their negotiations with trade unions. Prominent members include CBS, NBC, News Corp/Fox, MGM, Sony Pictures, the Walt Disney Company, and Warner Bros.

Industry Events

Television professionals have opportunities to gather throughout the year to network and learn about developments in the industry. Every union and trade organization has its own annual conferences. Some events include:

➤ Future of Television, sponsored by Digitalmediawire. This conference looks at the changes wrought by new technology and how it affects the television industry. (http://www.televisionconference.com)

➤ NAB Show, an event showcasing developments in digital media. This conference is attended by entertainment, media, and communications professionals who want to learn about the next generation of video and audio content and its application across multiple platforms. (http://www.nabshow.com)

➤ NATPE Convention. This annual conference is the largest gathering of syndicated television professionals. Industry professionals and advertisers gather here to plot the upcoming year of television programming. (http://www.natpe.org/conference)

Issues of Law and Government Regulation

Television, like other areas of the entertainment industry, is subject to many regulatory codes and ratings systems. These ensure content is geared toward appropriate audiences, as well as monitor the actions of media conglomerates.

Federal Communications Laws

The Communications Act of 1934, 47 U.S. Code Section 151 *et seq.*, gives the United States federal government control over all channels of radio and television broadcast. This law created the Federal

Communication Commission, giving it the power to grant licenses to television stations.

The Telecommunications Act of 1996, signed by President Bill Clinton, was the first major revision of telecommunications law since the Communications Act of 1934. The act updated the process by which stations were issued licenses, made provisions for the future advent of digital television broadcasting, and addressed satellite broadcasting services.

Title V of the Act concerns the regulation of obscene and violent programming on cable television. It made provisions for allowing parents to regulate the programs shown in their homes with the "V-Chip" and addressed the refusal of cable operators to carry some programs. (The "V" in "V-Chip" stands either for "violence" or "viewer control," depending on whom you ask.)

Critics of the Telecommunications Act have observed that although it was ostensibly intended to foster competition within the telecommunications industry, it has in fact resulted in a great reduction in the number of major media companies.

Federal Communications Commission (FCC)

The FCC is an independent government agency that regulates interstate and international communications by television, cable, satellite, wire, and radio. The FCC has jurisdiction over communications among all 50 states, Washington, DC, and all United States possessions. The organization is headed by five commissioners who are appointed by the president and confirmed by the United States Senate. The president chooses one of these commissioners to serve as chairperson of the FCC. Only three commissioners can be members of the same political party.

The commissioners direct the operations of the FCC's seven bureaus and staff offices. The bureaus and offices process applications for licenses, develop regulations, and conduct investigations and hearings. The different bureaus and offices each have their own specialties as well. The Consumer and Governmental Affairs Bureau, for example, coordinates telecommunications policy with various governments and industry and educates consumers about telecommunications. The Media Bureau regulates all television and radio stations.

One of the FCC's goals is to promote competition and diversity among the nation's media outlets. Competition is meant to encourage

Fast Facts

During 2004, FCC fines and settlements resulted in broadcasters paying over $11 million to the federal government. This was the year of the infamous Janet Jackson "wardrobe malfunction" that occurred during the halftime show of the Super Bowl; singer Justin Timberlake ripped open Jackson's top, exposing her right breast and raising the ire of millions of viewers. As it happened, the $11 million that the FCC took that year did not include a fine against CBS for this incident. The FCC tried to fine CBS $550,000 for the "malfunction." CBS appealed the ruling, and for several years it appeared that CBS would win the case. In 2009, however, the U.S. Supreme Court revisited the incident and sent the case back to a lower court to reconsider its decision and likely impose the full fine on the network.

innovation and create a wide variety of offerings for consumers. Promoting diversity is intended to make it possible for all people to have access to telecommunications products and opportunities, regardless of race, sex, national origin, or religion. Diversity is an area of some controversy; some groups believe that the FCC has not done all that it can to ensure that stations hire minorities as staffers or that a wide range of ethnicities are represented in television programming.

Though it may not seem obvious at the moment, the FCC's primary reason for existence is to facilitate the national defense and to keep people safe through wire and radio communications. The FCC still uses television and radio networks to communicate with large numbers of people during emergencies. This is why the federal government continues to invest in modernizing the nation's telecommunications infrastructure, including the transition to digital media; it wants the system to be reliable, easily repaired, and redundant (i.e., having many different resources that do the same job or produce the same product). It also wants all parts of the system to work with all other parts.

From a television business standpoint, the FCC's most important roles are its ability to grant licenses to television stations and to fine stations for broadcasting inappropriate content. In issuing licenses, the agency considers market coverage and ownership within a market. For example, in a market that has fewer than eight independently owned television stations, no single owner can own more than one of those stations. The FCC's objective is to increase competition and improve quality of programming. During the first decade of the twentieth century the FCC became more lax about insisting on a large number of owners, and the total number of station owners in the United States decreased. Stations must renew their licenses every three years.

FCC and Obscenity

In terms of programming content, the FCC issues regulations about what television stations can broadcast and when. In particular, it is worried about stations broadcasting material that is either indecent or obscene. (The FCC does not regulate violence in any way.)"Indecent" material is programming that contains sexual or excretory material but is not explicit enough to be considered obscene. "Profane language" is language so offensive that its mere utterance may be considered a legal "nuisance." "Obscenity" is material that an average person would find "appeals to prurient interests," depicts sexual content in a patently offensive way, and lacks serious literary, artistic, political, or scientific value. Defining all these terms is very much a matter of context, and broadcasters do not always know ahead of time what will stir the FCC's ire. In some cases, the FCC will revoke a station's license.

Federal law prohibits obscene programming at all times, and indecent or profane programming at hours when children are likely to be watching, generally from 6 A.M. until 10 P.M. Between 10 P.M. and 6 A.M. is a period of time known as the "safe harbor," in which stations may air indecent and profane material. Section 326 of the Communications Act prohibits the FCC from censoring program content or interfering with the free speech of broadcasters. This means that the FCC cannot review content ahead of time, but can only respond to complaints after the fact. If a station does broadcast inappropriate content, the FCC can fine it several thousand dollars per violation.

The FCC typically only enforces its indecency and profanity rules against conventional broadcast stations and networks, not cable or satellite stations. The anti-obscenity rules, however, apply to all television programming suppliers.

Of course, the First Amendment of the United States Constitution protects the right to free speech. This means that the FCC must constantly balance the rights to free speech with its interest in protecting the public from obscenity. In April 2009, the United States Supreme Court upheld the FCC's authority to regulate "fleeting expletives" in the case *FCC v. Fox Tel. Stations, Inc.* This case involved two shows in which performers uttered obscenities that were not written into pre-approved scripts, i.e. during live awards shows shown during prime time. After the event, the FCC issued new regulations forbidding fleeting expletives, retroactively finding that those shows had been in violation of its rules. Critics objected that the FCC had not followed its own prescribed procedure to change the rules and that it had not explained why it made the change. The Court's majority, however, held that the FCC had not acted arbitrarily and that its interest in preventing obscenity gave it the power to make rules as it saw fit.

Everyone Knows

Many people believe that the FCC wants to limit or ban religious programming. According to the FCC, this is a myth. Back in 1974, the FCC received a petition asking it to investigate the operating practices of stations licensed to religious organizations. The FCC denied this petition, but somehow a rumor started that well-known atheist Madalyn Murray O'Hair was behind an effort to ban religious television. Ever since then the FCC has received a regular stream of letters and telephone calls asking about this. The FCC insists that there is no basis for this belief, and that it in fact has no legal authority to ban religious programming on television or radio.

V-chip and TV Parental Guidelines

V-chip technology allows viewers to block certain channels, based on their ratings. The main users are parents who want to prevent their children from watching shows with profanity, violence, or sexual content. Since 2000 all new television sets sold in the United States have been equipped with the V-chip.

The V-chip blocks programs based on the TV Parental Guidelines system, which went into effect in 1997. Under this system, programs are given ratings based on the age of their intended audiences and the amount of "mature content" they contain. The ratings range from TV-Y, aimed at children under the age of seven, to TV-MA, intended only for mature audiences (i.e., viewers over the age of 16).

The ratings are:

- ➜ TV-Y (all children): denotes a program designed specifically for a very young audience, between two and six years
  old, and that is not expected to frighten young children.
- ➜ TV-Y7 (older children): denotes a program aimed at children seven and above. Programs may include mild fantasy, comic violence, and programs that require viewers
  to distinguish between fantasy and reality.
- ➜ TV-G (general audience): programs most parents would
  find suitable for all ages, including younger children.
  Programs contain little or no violence, sex, or strong
  language.
- ➜ TV-PG (parental guidance suggested): denotes programs
  that contain material that may be unsuitable for younger
  children due to moderate violence, sexual situations,
  infrequent coarse language, or suggestive dialogue.
- ➜ TV-14 (parents strongly cautioned): identifies programs
  that most parents would find unsuitable for children
  under the age of 14, due do intense violence, intense
  sexual situations, strong coarse languages, or intensely
  suggestive dialogue.
- ➜ TV-MA (mature audiences only): denotes programs that
  are unsuitable for children under 17 because they contain
  graphic sex or violence or crude indecent language.

These ratings have had mixed effects on programming. The guidelines have no legal force and participation is strictly voluntary. Some
advertisers avoid placing commercials in programs with TV-MA ratings, which has led some broadcasters to censor language in such
shows. The guidelines do not apply to news or sports programming.

Chapter 3

On the Job

Television can furnish jobs for all types of people. If you like to manage things, there is a job for you. If you prefer to design things, you can find employment. Perhaps you like to perform—television may furnish the perfect career. Or maybe you like to handle machinery, in which case you may enjoy the technical side of television production. This chapter describes some of the jobs available to those who work in television. It is divided into four sections, each containing alphabetical listings of the jobs within them:

1. *Administration and Management* covers positions on the production side, ranging from the lowly Production Assistant to the exalted Showrunner.
2. *Artistic* covers the people who create the actual television show that viewers see and hear. Directors, designers, and various artists fall under this category.
3. *On the Screen* covers people who work in front of the camera: actors, performers, and news broadcasters.
4. *Technical* covers the people who work with the machines and electronics that make television a reality.

These divisions are not the only possible ways of dividing up television jobs. You can also divide positions into those that happen before and during filming a show and those that happen after shooting. There is a good deal of overlap among areas regardless of how they are divided.

One important thing to remember about working in the television industry is that most jobs are short-term temporary positions, and most people working are freelance. That means that there is often no clear road from position to position. People do tend to specialize, and there are some fairly typical job paths, but because every job requires a new job search, people are not exactly being "promoted" as they move up in the hierarchy.

Administration and Management

Getting a show put together before it airs takes the cooperation of hundreds of people. If a producer pitches a show, market researchers will have to investigate its likelihood of success. Account executives will sell advertising for it. A casting director puts together a cast, and then perhaps shooting can begin. At that point even more people may get involved. Assistant directors, line producers, and floor managers all work together to make the show a reality.

Though there is no single path to success in this area, most people start out as lowly production assistants, or PAs. A PA may then work her way up to assistant director, producer, and maybe eventually become an exalted executive producer, also known as a showrunner.

Account Executive

Do you like meeting new people, going out to lunch and dinner, and talking on the telephone? Are you persuasive? Then you might make a good television account executive. An account executive sells advertising time, which is the main or only source of income for the majority of television stations and networks. Account executives are salespeople. They must constantly work to keep the stream of advertising revenue coming in. That requires maintaining relationships with existing clients, finding new sponsors, working with production to fit advertising spots into programming, and collecting payments for ads. As with many sales jobs, television stations often pay account executives at least partially through commissions. Energetic account executives can make very good money.

Assistant Director (AD)

An assistant director is often put in charge of managing the cast of a television show, especially the extras. An AD will also communicate with crew and makeup, wardrobe, and props. An assistant director is not a "director in training." Though it is not impossible for an assistant director to become a director, the position of assistant director is not considered a direct path to a directorship. Assistant directors generally serve more on the administrative and management side of production rather than the creative side. A typical job path finds one beginning as a Second Assistant Director, then moving up to First Assistant Director and finally Unit Production Manager.

Casting Director

The casting director is in charge of finding the cast of a television production. This can be a very time-consuming task. The casting director must read the script and meet with the director, writer, and producer to decide what sort of people they envision for each role. He or she then sifts through dozens, hundreds, or even thousands of actors to find the right ones. This process may include auditions, interviews, and negotiations with agents. The casting director also handles contracts with actors. A good casting director knows the names and faces of a huge number of performers and their agents, and is good at finding out whether or not they are available. A casting director also needs to be able to tell whether a performer will be good at a role; this includes both looking right for the part and having the necessary acting ability. Because the job requires so many connections and so much skill, casting directors usually have years of experience working in television or film. If you want to get into this area, try to find a job as a production assistant or casting associate for a casting director—and learn all you can about performers!

Floor Manager

A television floor manager organizes operations on the production floor, which is the main production area where a program's action occurs. This can be a stage in a studio or a temporary area erected in an outside filming location. Before a show, the floor manager helps plan productions, especially logistics, coordinates rehearsals, makes sure that furniture, props, and necessary equipment are in place, and briefs actors, presenters, and live audiences on what to expect. During shooting the floor manager wears an earpiece and microphone in order to transmit information between the director, control room, floor staff, and performers. He or she tells the director what is happening off camera, prepares performers for their cues and cues them when they need to appear on stage, and keeps the audience under control. Usually a person becomes a floor manager after a number of years of production experience. The floor manager needs to know what a show needs, how all the staff positions (such as lighting, sound, and camera) work, have an excellent sense of timing, and work well under pressure.

General Manager/Station Manager

A general manager runs a television station. This job includes monitoring sales of advertising, marketing the station, and filling airtime with good content. People generally become general manager after years of working in television. In broadcast television, it is not uncommon to move into the general manager role after working as a news director.

Market Research Analyst

Every television network wants to know how many people are going to watch its programs. Networks set advertising prices based on projected audiences, and advertisers get very unhappy if predictions do not meet with reality. So how do networks determine who will watch what shows? They employ market research analysts to find out. Analysts gather information on consumers through surveys done over the telephone, on the Internet, or person-to-person. They may also conduct focus groups in which groups of consumers watch a new program and then say what they think of it. They then compile this information, evaluate it, and use it to make recommendations to the networks about what people want to watch. If they do their job well, their predictions come true,

Fast Facts

You may have heard the expression "on the cutting room floor." That turn of phrase comes from the days when all television programs and movies were shot on film. When an editor removed a scene from a film, he or she literally cut that section of film out of the reel and dropped it on the floor. Today more editing is done in front of computer monitors—but editors still cut scenes all the time.

audiences love the shows they are supposed to, and advertisers get tons of exposure for their products. Most market researchers have at least a bachelor's degree, and many have advanced degrees. This is a growing field because companies are finding it ever harder to sell their products and want to target their advertising as precisely as possible.

News Director

A television news director runs a newsroom. This includes hiring and firing staffers, setting budgets, and directing and coordinating daily activities in the newsroom. The news director must come up with ideas for stories, review ideas that journalists propose, assign stories, monitor developing stories, and review edited news films and scripts. The news director is the one ultimately responsible for the content of news broadcasts and must ensure that everything that is broadcast follows station policy. To become a news director, you will need several years experience working in broadcast journalism. You will need to know a great deal about gathering news, creating stories, videography, and film editing. You will also need to good at interacting with other people, communicate well, and work well under pressure.

News Writer

Newsrooms often employ writers to write up stories for announcers to read on the air. Most news writers do not report their own stories. Instead they perform research in the studio's offices and write up news stories using that research combined with facts gathered by reporters in the field. The work is fast-paced. This is a good area for someone who likes current events, can write quickly, and who might like to move into a bigger position in television news.

Producer

A producer controls all the aspects of producing a television show. This starts with identifying good ideas and continues through writing scripts, casting performers, shooting, and final editing. The producer is in charge of the show's budget. The producer may also be a writer on the show; the person credited as "producer" for an episode is often the person who served as head writer on that episode. Most shows have a number of different producers, who may handle different responsibilities. A coproducer helps produce a script for an episode or show but is not the main writer. A segment producer is in charge of the writing and possibly the production of one portion of a program. A supervising producer may supervise lower-ranking producers and writers. An executive producer, or showrunner, is the producer in charge of the entire operation. A consulting producer acts as a consultant, occasionally assisting the writers. Line producers and coordinating producers (production coordinators). One possible path through the ranks of production would be going from production assistant to line producer, segment producer, producer, and finally executive producer or showrunner.

Production Coordinator

A production coordinator, or coordinating producer, handles the schedule and staffing of a show. This can include forming staff members into teams and arranging leadership for them, giving assignments to production assistants, posting call times for staff and cast, and anything else that needs to be coordinated to make a show happen. A good production coordinator looks at the big picture, decides

Fast Facts

D-Girl

A d-girl, or a development girl, is an entry-level worker in a film or television production company who works on finding and developing new scripts. Most d-girls are female, as you might expect, but the term may also be used for men who perform the same job. A d-girl reads scripts that are sent to the company and writes summaries of them for the producers, and also looks for new ideas that could be developed into scripts. The title *d-girl* is somewhat derogatory, indicating a junior executive with no real power. Though many people learned about the term's negative connotations in an episode of the HBO series *The Sopranos*, this is not a bad position for someone who aims to move into the realm of production.

what has to be done when, and heads off problems before they start. Some production coordinators find themselves wearing a variety of different hats, from helping write scripts to casting extras to finding a good source for cheap props.

Line Producer (Unit Production Manager)

Are you a good at organizing and running things? You might make a good line producer. The line producer is responsible for all the practical details of producing a television show, as opposed to the artistic or technical details. The line producer oversees daily operations, including watching the budget, hiring crews, ordering food from caterers, and making sure that everyone who needs to communicate is communicating. The line producer also makes sure that postproduction processes such as editing and special effects get incorporated at the right time. The line producer must be very organized, good with numbers, be able to coordinate multiple tasks simultaneously, and be a good leader. Patience and the ability to stay calm in the face of what may appear to be chaos are both key qualities. If you are the line producer, everyone involved in the show will be looking to you to reassure them that everything is going well; staying calm is the best way to keep everyone else calm.

Location Manager

Many television shows shoot scenes in a number of different locations, not just on a single set. For example, an episode of a drama may include scenes on a highway, in the woods, in a field, at a boathouse, and in a shopping mall. The location manager's job is to find places that would be perfect for those scenes and arrange to shoot there. To find locations, the location manager uses location scouts, people who travel around looking for places to shoot. The location manager then selects the best of those and handles the legal and logistical aspects of shooting there, including getting permission from property owners and filing for permits. Most location managers have experience working as a location scout.

Location Scout

A location scout works for a location manager, finding perfect places to shoot scenes. A location scout may spend most of his or her day driving around looking at places. Location scouts have to consider the appearance of a site, available lighting, logistics such as weather, parking, electricity, and other facilities, and convenience for shooting. A location manager typically wants the scouts to find several possible locations for each scene so that the production will have some options. This is a great job for someone who likes to be on the move and enjoys meeting lots of new people all the time.

Production Assistant (PA)

A production assistant, also known as a PA or gopher (as in "go for this or that"), is an entry-level grunt worker on a television production. Production assistants spend hours working for little pay, doing all the odd jobs that need doing. These jobs can include making copies, driving people to and from the airport, organizing notes, getting coffee, and anything else one of the more exalted workers needs done. Any member of the production team can ask the production assistant to do nearly anything. The job can be either very stressful, as many people place demands on the PA, or very educational, as the PA gets to experience the full range of television production tasks. Production assistants do not need any particular educational background; what is more important is that they are good listeners, energetic, show up on time, and never refuse any task. Many successful television producers got their starts as production assistants, which makes this a great place to begin a television career.

Researcher

Do you like to investigate topics? Are you good at finding information on the Internet or in the library? Then you may enjoy working as a television researcher. All types of television productions employ researchers to investigate program topics. Researchers may come up with ideas for shows, check facts within scripts, and brief writers on various matters so that their scripts will be accurate. Researchers may also investigate shooting locations, look for sources of old footage, and find experts who can contribute to productions either as consultants or as participants in a show. Some production companies have their researchers take care of compliance with copyrights and other legal requirements. After a production is completed, a researcher may be put in charge of creating publicity materials, press releases, Web site content, and similar materials used to promote the program.

Showrunner/Executive Producer

The showrunner is the person who runs a television show. In many cases that person is the head writer, the person who controls the creative direction of a program. A television series showrunner is frequently the person who created the series. The executive producer is often considered the showrunner; frequently the executive producer and head writer are the same person. But a showrunner does more than just write scripts and head the creative team; a showrunner can hire and fire writers and crew, cast actors, negotiate with studios and networks, and set budgets. The showrunner is the overall boss; in the world of television, the showrunner frequently outranks the director.

Statistics Person

Do you like sports? Are you decent at math? Stats may be the place for you. The statistics person, or statistics recorder, finds relevant statistical information and conveys it to the presenters or the audience or enters it into a computer system where other staff members can find it. To accomplish this task, the stats person must watch the game very carefully and think quickly. A statistics person must know a lot about the subject matter, including the rules of the game, the meaning of referee calls, the names of important players, and ideally something about the recent history of the game.

Television Writer

A television writer creates scripts for television programs. This process can include creating plot lines, inventing characters, and writing dialogue. Individual writers may specialize in comedy, drama, or documentary productions. Television writers often work in teams; this is particularly true for television series that produce new episodes every week. There are several levels of writer. Staff writers are the newest writers, usually with less than two years' experience. Story editors and executive story editors are more experienced, and may be put in charge of teams of writers. A producer may be a head writer. A segment producer is a writer who writes one segment of a show.

Writers may move up through the ranks to become producers. The best way to get into television writing is to do a lot of writing. Television producers hire writers based on their portfolios; new writers must usually submit "spec" script, a sample script for a show that already exists using existing characters and plotlines in a sensible way. If you want to enter this field, the best preparation you can do is to read and watch a lot a television and films, paying attention to the way stories and dialogue are constructed. Then practice writing; it can take a long time to get the feel for writing dialogue, so a lot of practice is worthwhile. There are also several writer training programs available. A typical path for a television writer is starting as a freelancer, then moving through the ranks of staff writer, story editor, executive story editor, executive story consultant, and finally showrunner.

Artistic

Actually creating a show requires the work of a number of artists. These include specialists in makeup, costumes, and hair styling, designers to create convincing sets and attractive lighting, and cinematographers who can compose beautiful shots. Controlling the whole operation is the director. After shooting is done, the editor takes the footages and cuts and splices it into a seamless whole.

Art Director Production Designer

Do you like art and design? When you read a book, do you imagine elaborate settings for the story? Then you might enjoy working as a production designer on a television program. The production designer, the head of the art department, is in charge of the way a show looks. He or she meets with the director and producer to determine the look of a production and then creates sketches or models that capture this vision. The next step is to organize the art department and crew to build the set or adapt the location. Becoming a production designer takes a lot of training and experience. You will need to study design for several years; many production designers have college degrees in design, architecture, or theatrical set design. Production designers often hire assistants; this can be a good way to find out if this career is right for you and get some tips on how to go about entering it.

Colorist

When a film gets to the editor, the color often looks very strange. Different lighting and different cameras can result in shots of the same scene looking very different from one another. The colorist's job is to make sure the color is consistent from frame to frame through a process called color correction. This job is done digitally today, but in the past it was done by hand. A colorist needs to understand photography, color theory, and be good with computers.

Continuity Director

The continuity director is in charge of ensuring that the scenes within a television program are consistent. Television shows and films are often shot out of order and scenes are typically shot from several different angles. In order to get a seamless show, all of the correct elements have to be in the scene every time it is shot, including props, costumes, hair styles, camera settings, environmental conditions, cast members, and anything else that a viewer could see. The continuity director keeps track of all of this information on a continuity report. That way the director can verify all details of a scene before shooting it. Continuity mistakes can be embarrassing if they are not caught, and reshooting a scene can be expensive and sometimes impossible, so the continuity director's job is very important.

Director

The director directs the actors in a television drama, telling them where to stand, when to move, and how to say their lines. Television actually uses two kinds of directors, multi-camera and single camera. A single camera production is like a movie; the director uses one camera at a time to get different shots that are later edited into a single show. This technique is common on made-for-television movies and television dramas that are shot in multiple areas. A multi-camera production uses multiple cameras (usually three) simultaneously to shoot a show or an event. This technique is typically used for talk shows, sporting events, news programs, and sitcoms.

A single camera director works very much like a movie director. The director will usually position himself or herself near the actors in order to give them direction more easily. Single-camera directors may have more time to work than multi-camera directors, but they still usually operate under tighter deadlines than movie directors. A multi-camera director of a sitcom may work down on the stage with the actors, but directors who work on live events usually spend their time in a video booth where they can see the images being shot on all the cameras. They can direct the camera operators to take close-ups or long shots in order to ensure that they have all footage necessary to put together a good show. Multi-camera directing of fast-paced events such as football games can be very stressful.

Director of Photography (DP)/Cinematographer

The director of photography heads up the camera department. When a director plans a show, he or she creates a list of scenes. The director of photography must decide how to set up and film those scenes. This includes deciding where to place cameras and lights, how to incorporate natural light, which cameras and filters to use, and how to deploy the camera crew so that they can capture as much of the scene as possible without getting in the way of the actors. The camera crew includes camera operators, lighting technicians, and all related assistants. After shooting, the director of photography must make sure the film or video has come out correctly. To become a director of photography, you will need to study all aspects of photography and lighting, and probably some art as well. Watching old movies is a great way to develop your eye for how to compose shots. Most good DPs have years of experience working on camera or lighting crews; photography skills take a long time to develop, and are best learned through practice and working with experts.

Editor

An editor, or video editor, arranges footage in the best order to tell a story or otherwise create a television program that flows smoothly and makes sense. Almost every show requires some degree of editing; even live shows need an editor to choose shots. Most productions end up with far more footage than can be used in a half-hour or one-hour program. It is the editor's job to watch all of this footage and then, using the director or producer's guidance, select clips and arrange them in the best possible order. There is a real art to assembling a program that flows logically; the best editors have almost a musical sense of timing and rhythm. Editors may also do basic tasks such as dubbing footage onto disks, archiving footage, or converting formats.

Foley Artist

A Foley artist is in charge of adding sounds to the soundtrack. Often a program is recorded with no sound at all; if it is recorded with sound, the microphones do not pick up all the sounds that the director or producer would like. The Foley artist adds sound effects such as the smack of a kiss, wind whistling through the trees, or the crack of bones breaking. Foley artists use many creative techniques to create sounds. To create the sound of a giant stepping on a person, a Foley artist might wrap a cabbage in ground meat and drop an anvil on it. Flapping gloves sound remarkably like birds flapping their wings in flight. To make the sound of horses' hooves, Foley artists really have tapped coconut shells together, as made famous in *Monty Python and the Holy Grail.*

Graphic Designer

A graphic designer creates visual images designed to convey messages. Graphic designers create images for all types of media, including print, Internet, and television. Television networks and stations use graphic designers to create logos, to design images for commercials and programs, and to design the opening and closing credits for programs. Graphic designers work by sketching initial designs, either by hand or on a computer, and then adding colors, sound, animation, and other visual elements. If you want to be a graphic designer, you will need to have good artistic skills, understand design principles, and be very good at working on a computer. You will also need to be able to keep working even if your designs are rejected or changed out of recognition with your original ideas.

Hair Stylist

A hair stylist styles the hair of performers before they appear on camera. The hair stylist may also work on set to touch up hair in between takes. Hair stylists usually learn their skills at a beauty school and then spend some years working as an apprentice in a salon. If you have experience doing hair, you can assemble a portfolio of your work to show to television production companies when you apply for jobs. Performers often develop passionate loyalty for their favorite hair stylists; if you can make a famous actor decide that your work is indispensible, you can have a very good career indeed!

Key Makeup Artist

The key makeup artist runs the makeup department. He or she designs the makeup for each performer and assigns makeup artists to carry out these designs. This includes deciding what cosmetic products to use, creating desired effects, and possibly using prostheses or other devices to enlarge noses and other tricks of the trade. This is a great job for someone who enjoys designing new looks and has real artistic skills. A large production may use a team of many artists and assistants, and the key makeup artist oversees them all. Key makeup artists, like other makeup artists, usually have a cosmetology degree and a number of years of experience. Many of them also have a background in art and color theory, important for making performers look good on the screen.

Key Wardrobe/Costume Supervisor

Do you like clothes? Do you have a good understanding of both current and historical fashions? Most importantly, do you love to shop, and are you good at finding bargains? If so, wardrobe may be the place for you. The key wardrobe person is the leader of the wardrobe on a television production. The key wardrobe person sometimes functions as costume designer, deciding how each character will look, and sometimes just makes the costume designer's ideas a reality. To do this, the key wardrobe person reads the script, studies the characters, and decides what sort of clothes would be right for each character. The key wardrobe then procures all of these clothes, either by buying them or by making them. Each garment must be fitted to the person who will wear it. During production, the key wardrobe person is responsible to getting the right costumes to the right actors, retrieving them after shooting is complete for the day, keeping track of where all costume pieces are at any given time, and keeping the garments clean and in good repair.

Lighting Director

A lighting director is in charge of the lighting of a television production. While television cameras can pick up images with very little light, television productions use a great deal of artificial light to make shots look better. The lighting director chooses which lights to use and where to place them in order to get the look that the show's director wants. This requires the lighting director to understand lights, shadows, and colors, and how to create flattering effects with light. The lighting director may use a light board to coordinate a number of different lights, turning them on and off or setting them to different levels as a production proceeds. The lighting director may supervise a crew of electricians who handle the technical aspects of installing and running lights. Some lighting directors also call themselves lighting designers, emphasizing the artistic side of their work.

Makeup Artist

Almost no performer appears on television without makeup. Actors in dramas wear makeup that helps them inhabit their roles; news announcers and presenters wear makeup that makes them look better. It is the job of the makeup artist to apply makeup to performers to make them look good on television. Depending on the size of the production, there may be multiple makeup artists, including a key makeup artist and several assistants. Many makeup artists start out by studying cosmetology and then working as an assistant. Starting pay for makeup artists is not great, and makeup artists work long hours, just like all television professionals. If you like art, cosmetics, and working very closely with people, though, this could be a good career for you.

Makeup Effects Artist

A makeup effects artist is no ordinary makeup artist. Instead of working exclusively with cosmetics, a makeup effects artist uses latex, prosthetics, and other devices to dramatically alter the appearance of actors. Any program that features fantasy characters or characters who are much older or fatter than the performers who portray them makes use of a makeup effects artist. If you go into this field, you may find yourself turning actors into aliens with latex ears and noses or helping a slender actress look pregnant through the addition of a prosthetic chin. If you are good at sculpture and chemistry (many people are allergic to glues or latex) you might enjoy this field.

Prop Master

The prop master handles the props, which are all the small movable items used on a set. These include pots and pans in a kitchen, books on a shelf, magazines on a coffee table, desk lamps, cigarettes and lighters, and any other items that a performer could pick up and carry around. The prop master works with the set designer to determine what props are necessary, acquires those props, arranges them on the set or gets them to the actor who will carry them onto the set, and puts them away after shooting is complete. The prop master also replaces or fixes any props that are broken or lost. A prop master must be extremely organized and resourceful to keep track of all the props and ensure that all the correct ones are in the right place at the right time. Prop masters work in television art departments; it is not unusual for prop masters to have some training in art and design.

Everyone Knows

There are definite hierarchies within the television industry. One way to differentiate people is through the gradations of their titles. Nearly every job in this chapter can be modified by adding the word "assistant" before or after it. A floor manager can have an assistant floor manager. Some people get jobs as assistant camera operators. Assume that any job can also come in an "assistant" version. Most assistants do what you would expect: They help the person with the main title. Assistants also come in gradations; first assistant outranks second assistant, who outranks third assistant. In the technical departments, the word "key" often denotes a worker with a supervisory role. A "key grip" is the top grip. The key wardrobe person is the wardrobe supervisor.

Set Decorator

The set decorator is in charge of making the set look right. This includes setting up furniture, choosing wallpaper and lamps, picking out and setting up lighting fixtures, and generally taking care of anything that an interior decorator might do in a house. The set decorator does not necessarily take care of props, though there can be overlap between the two areas.

Wardrobe Assistant/Costumer

A wardrobe assistant works in the wardrobe of a television production, supervised by the key wardrobe person. A wardrobe assistant helps choose and acquire costumes, fit them on the performers who will wear them, and take care of them between shoots. To get a job as a wardrobe assistant, it is very helpful to have some skill in sewing and to have a very good eye for fashion. Some courses in fashion design will not hurt, though they may not be necessary. Wardrobe assistants often work their way up to head wardrobe departments, where they can be very well paid for their expertise.

On the Screen

Some of the most glamorous jobs in television are on the screen. Actors and performers can attract millions of fans and make tremendous sums of money. There are openings for on-screen personalities at all types of television stations; local broadcast news is a great place to start a career on camera. Be warned, though: The competition is fierce, and only the most persistent souls make it.

Actor

Actors are the people who play the roles of characters on television shows. They must learn lines, practice movements, wear makeup and costumes, and then convince viewers that they are other people. Most television actors have some training in acting, and many of them have college degrees in theatre or television and film studies. Even successful actors may continue perfecting their art through actors' workshops. (A few succeed through talent alone, but this is uncommon; if you are serious about acting, putting in the time to study acting theory and technique will only help you.) Successful actors belong to the Screen Actors' Guild (SAG), which guarantees certain levels of pay and can help actors get jobs. Most actors work in Los Angeles or New York.

Anchor

An anchor, also called an anchorwoman, anchorman, or anchorperson, is the lead newscaster on a news program. The anchor opens and closes the news broadcast, reads reports, introduces reports from other journalists, and interviews visitors to the news program. When they are not on camera, anchors spend their work time reading wire services and reports and writing scripts for the day's newscasts. Anchors have to be ready to change gear at a moment's notice; if a major event occurs, all scripts go out the window and the anchor must improvise on the air with only the producer's voice speaking over an earpiece to help. Anchors generally get their jobs after years of television reporting. The job is high profile so anchors must pay close attention to personal grooming, including wearing makeup on camera. Working as an anchor at a major station can be very lucrative, but most anchor jobs at small stations are not especially well paid.

Announcer

An announcer is a performer who speaks on the air. There is a good deal of variation in that job title. Announcers who work for news programs appear on the air to read news reports and interview guests. Sports announcers provide commentary during sporting events. Some announcers specialize in doing voice-over work, recording their voices on top of existing footage; this is very common in television commercials. Station identification announcements are done by announcers who may never appear on screen. Announcers must have strong, clear voices, good diction, excellent reading skills, and may also need to be able to improvise as needed. Announcers and anchors who work in studios read most of their spoken content from Teleprompters that display scripts written by news writers. Announcers and anchors may write their own scripts before they go on the air. Many people become announcers after working as reporters in the field. Others enter the field with specialized training in some desirable field, such as meteorology or economics.

Entertainer

Television entertainers are people who perform on television as themselves, not as actors portraying other characters. This category includes singers, celebrity chefs, comedians, and a host of other performers who have managed to parlay some skill into an entertainment career. Many of the individuals who work as television entertainers essentially invented themselves. For example, a cooking show might come about because an individual chef creates a concept for a television program and then sells it to a network. If you have developed your skills in a certain area, have a good look for television, and do not mind talking before an audience, you might be able to find work as an entertainer.

Extra

An extra, or background artist, is a performer who appears on screen but does not have an official role in the production. Television programs and movies often need large numbers of people to populate their settings. For example, a scene set at a football game would look strange without fans sitting in the stands. A city street would not look realistic without lots of people walking around. It would be very expensive to find actual actors for these roles, so studios hire extras. Extras do not speak and get very little glory. Often their faces are not even visible. But working as an extra is one way to break into acting, and one of the known paths into the Screen Actors' Guild (SAG). Pay for nonunion extras is not very high, but SAG members who work as extras make a decent pay. Extras never know what to expect from their next job; if you work as an extra, you may play a college student one day and an alien the next. Working as an extra entails long days of waiting around; be sure to bring a book or some other type of personal entertainment!

Foreign Correspondent

A foreign correspondent is a journalist who gathers news in a distant location and sends reports back to his or her home network or station. Foreign correspondents cover a variety of topics, from royal weddings and international fashion shows to foreign wars. A foreign correspondent often supplies some context or personal experience in his or her reporting. This job can be glamorous, involving foreign travel and attending high-profile events. It can also be lonely and quite dangerous. Foreign correspondents must leave their homes and families on a regular basis to pursue stories in distant lands. Sometimes they are literally in the line of fire. During the Iraq war, embedded reporters actually stayed with troops to catch the details of the fighting. If this field interest you, you will need to be a top-notch journalist, and you will probably need to be fluent in at least one foreign language.

Everyone Knows

Good makeup artists are highly valued. Many famous actors have favorite makeup artists who they believe make them look especially good, and they will request their favorites when they agree to work on a television or film project.

Host

A host, emcee, or presenter, serves as the face and voice of a television program. Hosts are commonly used for game shows, talk shows, children's programs, home shopping networks, and awards shows. Celebrities typically hold this position, so if you are interested in hosting a television show your best bet is to work on becoming famous. Children's programming is an exception. Many children's shows like to use young hosts, which gives youthful newcomers an opportunity to enter the field and make their names. Television hosts must be attractive, well-spoken, confident, and good at thinking on their feet. Improvisation is a big part of this job. Sometimes a host wears an earpiece to hear instructions from the director or producer; this makes it more challenging to converse naturally on stage.

Reporter

A television reporter creates news stories for television broadcasts. Reporters find leads, gather information, assemble that information into coherent narratives, and record final broadcasts. The job includes contacting and interviewing subjects, keeping up-to-date on events and information, writing scripts, and speaking in front of the camera, often on the scene of the story. The pace can be fast and hours long; reporters often find that they have barely enough time to complete a story before going live with it. Some television reporters specialize in a particular area, such as crime, city hall, science, or consumer news. Foreign correspondents film stories in remote locations, where they may be challenged by language and cultural differences and endangered by wars and violence.

Technical

Producing television programs requires the use of a great deal of equipment. Technicians transport, set up, run, and fix all sorts of different machines, from sound mixing boards to steadicams. This is a great field for someone who likes to work with electronics and who is not confused by masses of cables. It is also a good area for people who enjoy combining technical work with art; every camera operator is an artist, and the best sound mixers have a very delicate touch with their work.

Best Boy

A best boy is a chief assistant in either the electric or the grip department. "Best boy electric" assists the gaffer, or head electrician. "Best boy grip" assists the key grip. Despite the name, a best boy can be female and is nearly always an adult. Best boys take care of day-to-day operations in their departments. Depending on the size of the crew, the best boy may be in charge of hiring and scheduling crew members, submitting timecards for workers, choosing equipment and loading trucks, setting up rigging or lighting at remote units, applying union rules, and coordinating production with the other departments involved in the show.

Cable Puller

A cable puller is one of the most junior television technicians. A cable puller takes care of cables. In many productions, the roving cameras are connected to the control room by cables. When a camera operator walks around with a camera, the cable is pulled along behind. It is the cable puller's job to walk around behind the camera holding the cable, making sure it does not get stuck, tangled, or present a tripping hazard. The cable puller does this by holding a section of cable coiled loosely in one hand and feeding it out with the other. The camera operator needs enough slack to move easily, but not so much that he risks tangling his feet in cable. The cable puller may also help the camera operator walk backward by placing a hand on the camera operator's back to serve as a guide. The bad news about working as a cable puller is that the pay is generally very low, or even non-existent; cable pullers are often interns or volunteers. The good news is that a cable puller really needs almost no qualifications or experience, so it is an excellent entry-level position for someone who wants to try working in television production.

CCU (Camera Control Unit) Operator

A CCU operator works in a camera control unit controlling cameras remotely. Typically the CCU operator will take care of technical details such as aperture, color balance, and shutter speed in order to ensure that multiple cameras produce compatible results and to allow the camera operators to concentrate on the artistic aspects of shooting such as composition. A CCU operator may control between three and ten cameras. Broadcasts involving many cameras may use several CCU operators. Sometimes a technical director works as a CCU operator; in other cases, the TD supervises CCU operators and works closely with them.

Camera Operator

A camera operator uses a film or video camera to capture footage. Field operators use portable cameras that they can set up to shoot at different locations. They may take footage back to the studio for later editing, or they may transmit the footage as a live transmission; this is often the case with news camera operators, who may travel with field presenters and sound operators in order to send complete transmissions directly to the television screen. Studio camera operators work as part of a studio camera team. Many studio productions are shot with several cameras at once. Each operator covers a portion of the action, and the director or an editor selects which shots end up in the broadcast. Camera operators need to know about both photography and videography, recognize basic types of shots, and understand the principles of video or film editing. Field camera work can be physically challenging because it involves lifting and setting up a fairly large camera on a regular basis.

Chief Engineer

The chief engineer is the head technician on a production. A chief engineer knows how to set up and operate all of the equipment needed to produce and broadcast a television show. The chief engineer supervises the other technicians, takes care of preventive maintenance of equipment, and knows how to respond to technical emergencies. Sometimes an engineer must work very quickly to solve problems in time for a program to appear. Skill in digital technology is becoming increasingly important in this field.

Electrician/Lighting Technician

An electrician is a technician who works with electrical equipment, primarily lights. Electricians are also called lighting technicians. The electricians set up the lights, install generators, run cables, color the lights with gels, and create effects. The technician called a gaffer, or chief lighting technician, heads the lighting department. The gaffer's assistant is sometimes called the "best boy." A career path in the electric department might begin with a post as an assistant electrician, moving up to an electrician, best boy, and eventually gaffer.

Gaffer/Chief Lighting Technician

The gaffer is the head of the electrical department. The gaffer works closely with the director of photography or lighting director to achieve desired lighting results. The lighting director or director of photography envisions the way the production will be lit, but it is up to the gaffer to decide how to make this vision come to life and to implement it. Gaffers need to know how to the technical aspects of how to work and set up different types of lights, how to use generators, and how to run cables, but they also need to understand the artistic side of lighting. Gaffers choose colored gels to tint lights in order to achieve different effects, such as the noonday sun glaring down on actors' heads or the soft light of a candle at a restaurant table. The gaffer works closely with the key grip, who handles the setup of cameras and some of the lights. Gaffers are usually quite experienced in the field and often own their own equipment, including a truck to carry it all. Gaffers often start out as technical assistants or cable pullers and gradually work their way up.

Grip

Grips are in charge of mounting and moving cameras on cranes or dollies. They also help set up lights. The "key grip" is the head grip. A dolly grip is in charge of mounting a camera on a moving cart called a dolly and moving it along its track during filming. The key grip's assistant is called a "best boy" (just like the chief assistant in the electrical department). A worker in the grip department may start as a cable puller, then work his or her way up to assistant grip, grip, and finally key grip.

Sound Operator/Sound Engineer

Sound operators are responsible for recording and mixing the sound used in television programs. Getting good sound is not a simple task. Sound engineers must know how to place microphones, which microphones to use in a given situation, and how to mix audio tracks so that everything that needs to be audible is. Some sound operators work in the field. When a sound operator goes out with a camera operator to shoot footage, he or she brings along an audio field kit that may contain lapel microphones, handheld microphones, boom microphones, headphones, a recorder, and a portable mixer. The sound operator will position mics as needed, including attaching lapel mics onto actors, monitor audio levels while shooting proceeds, and make sure that the audio track is being recorded. Within a studio, a sound operator will also be responsible for choosing and placing microphones, but may sit at a large mixing board while shooting goes on. A mixing board allows the technician to allocate each source of sound to a different channel and to mix them all together in an audio feed. This can be a very complicated job that requires a fair amount of technical skill.

Steadicam Operator

A steadicam is a camera on a stabilizing mount that keeps the camera steady even if the operator moves with it, unlike a standard camera, which will produce jerky footage if the camera moves. Steadicams are used for scenes in which the camera operator must move quickly with the action; the NBC television series *ER* was famous for its long steadicam shots of events taking place throughout a hospital emergency room. A steadicam operator wears a harness that supports the camera. The work is physical and requires a fair amount of training in camera operation. Steadicams are bulky and heavy, and although cameras have gotten smaller over the years, newer high definition cameras are still big. For that reason, steadicams are often now mounted on cranes, cars, helicopters, and other devices that can move with the action.

Technical Director (TD)

In general, the technical director is in charge of the technical side of a television production. The TD chooses equipment and oversees its preparation, plans the technical details of shooting and postproduction, selects and trains staff, helps choose camera settings and lenses, and solves technical problems that occur during production. The TD may also operate a vision switcher or CCU controller, running equipment that controls camera functions such as aperture so that the camera operators can focus on composing shots. The TD keeps track of all video sources and keeps them at broadcast quality. If you want to work as a technical director, you will have to know all about camera operation, CCU control, and the other technical aspects of production. A solid background in electronics would definitely be useful in this field.

Technician/Engineer

Technicians are in charge of setting up, running, and taking care of technical equipment involved in television production. A broadcast technician sets up and operates electronic equipment used to broadcast a television production and regulate the strength and clarity of broadcast signals. Audio equipment technicians set up sound equipment, including microphones, speakers, amplifiers, mixing boards, and recording equipment. Audio equipment technicians handle video cameras, screens, projectors, and monitors. Technicians often can operate many different types of equipment. This is a good job for someone who enjoys working with cables, wires, and all types of electronics.

Videotape (VT) Director

A VT director works in large television production units that use multiple videotape machines and VT operators. The VT director works with the main program director of a program to decide what sources to record on machines and which replays to include in the program, and then coordinates the playback of videotaped material during the production of the program. These days content may be on computer-based systems instead of strictly videotape; part of the VT operator's job is to understand the recording systems availableThe machines are usually kept in a room other than the control room, or outside in a truck. The VT director must know how to operate the machines (VT directors often find themselves operating one or more VT machines), be good at directing staff members, and understand the subject matter and other requirements of the program in question. VT directors must be confident in their ability to act quickly and often must make quick decisions about what content to play. This job can be stressful, but may appeal to you if you like to think on your feet.

Videotape (VT) Operator

A VT operator records and plays back video material, using a videotape machine, a computer-based system, or other mechanism. A VT operator's duties may include making a master tape of a program, creating slow motion replays, editing video footage, and cueing and playing video clips at the right time in a program. This job can be very easy or very difficult, depending on the needs of the production. A VT operator working in a postproduction editing session may need only to be able to find video clips, play them, and record them. A VT operator working in a large production unit on a live production may need to think and act very quickly to play the right clips at exactly the right moments. VT operators work under a VT director or under a main production editor. A VT operator needs to know how to use different types of video equipment, including editing software.

Chapter 4

Tips for Success

There are many career paths in the television industry, all quite different from one another. This chapter deals with getting into various aspects of the industry in different sections. But all people who work in television agree on certain keys to success.

1. Network. You will get jobs through the people you know.
2. Be on time.
3. Be willing to work long hours.
4. If the only job offered you is a lowly production assistant position, take it!
5. Be polite.
6. Keep trying!

If you remember these six points, you will be well ahead of much of your competition. It goes without saying that you need to be good at what you do, whatever your specialty is, but there are and always will be tons of people who are just as good. But if you can make yourself stand out through your connections and your diligence, you will have a better chance of getting good jobs and moving up. And keep trying; if you knock on enough doors, one of them is bound to open eventually.

Number One Tip: Networking

Networking, or making and using contacts with other people for job purposes, may be the single most important thing you can do to make your television career successful.

Career counselors tell their clients that most jobs are never advertised at all. Most jobs get filled by networking, or word-of-mouth. This is especially true of jobs in television; busy television execs simply do not have the time to sift through résumés. But networking is not just useful for finding jobs. A good network can facilitate nearly anything you try to do.

Do you need a job? Talk to friends and acquaintances who either work where you want to work or might know someone who does. Do you need help performing a task? Ask someone you think might know how; even if he or she cannot help you, you may find out who can. Do you want to work on a television drama? Go to parties or events where you can meet people involved with it. Some networking can happen accidentally. Maybe you decide to take a sailing class, and who should share a boat with you but one of the key grips you wanted to meet! Now the two of you are friends, and maybe he will think of you if he needs an assistant.

Anyone can form part of your network—family, friends, acquaintances, and friends of friends. That is one good reason to always be polite; you never know when an acquaintance might help be able to help you or when you might be able to help an acquaintance.

One difficulty with networking is that television professionals often change jobs. You may work five months for one show, take a short break, do eight months at another show, and then find yourself in need of a job. By this time there may be an opening for you at your first show, but the people working there have forgotten you. Try to keep in touch with your old contacts as much as you can.

Hit the East or West Coast

There are television jobs everywhere. Most cities of any decent size have local stations that offer some employment opportunities. Some cities, such as Atlanta, employ hundreds of people in television, both through local stations and at the giant news network CNN. The truth is, though, that the majority of jobs are in New York and Los Angeles. If you are serious about working in television and you can manage to move to one of those cities, you should do it. You will maximize your chances of meeting the right people and forming a solid network, you will be near auditions and shooting locations, and you will be surrounded by classes, agents, and other useful institutions.

Keeping
in Touch

These tips for success apply to people in most areas, but they are especially applicable to the television field:

1. Be on time. Does that seem obvious? You would be amazed how many people have difficulty with punctuality. Television deadlines come fast and furious. Broadcasts have to happen exactly on the hour or half hour. If the studio is ready to shoot but you are not there in costume to make your appearance, or you have not handed in a complete script, no one will be happy.

2. Return your phone calls and e-mails. Sure, everyone in entertainment is tethered to a Blackberry or iPhone, but a lot of those people are not actually communicating with anyone. Returning calls is an easy way to set yourself apart from the crowd.

3. Always be polite. Being courteous to superiors can get you better assignments. Being courteous to those who work for you will get you better work. And it's so much nicer to be in a workplace where people are polite to one another.

4. Say thank you. If someone does you a favor, thank him or her! After you interview for a job, send notes to the people who took the time to talk to you thanking them for doing so. If an assistant director hires you as an extra for a day, send a thank you note. Not only will it make them like you better, it will also remind them of your existence.

5. Mind your grammar. Bad grammar looks unprofessional. You may be texting all the time, but you will also have to write actual e-mails or even formal documents. (You may think your e-mail grammar does not matter, but there are many readers who think otherwise and will look down on you if you do not bother with capitals or punctuation.) Just think of it as one more easy way to set yourself apart from the crowd.

Join the Union

Television and film production are heavily unionized industries. If you want to work in television, you will need to join the union that governs your area of expertise.

Television: An Industry for the Young

The average age of people working in television is slightly lower than that of people in other industries. Why is this? It is simple: Anyone who works in television must contend with long hours, low pay, and tremendous job uncertainty. Young people tend to be more willing to put up with those conditions than older people.Many people spend their twenties working in television, but switch to more stable employment when they want to start their families.

There have been suggestions that the television industry also discriminates against older workers because of a perpetual desire to attract younger viewers, the favorite demographic of advertisers. In 2000 a group of television writers sued a number of media companies alleging that the networks stopped hiring them to write scripts after they turned 40 years old. Some networks explicitly say that they do not hire writers over a certain age. Actors, especially female ones, often find it harder to get roles once they pass 30 or so; after all, there are always younger actors offering their services, and television stations like to cast young, bright faces. The problem is not quite as pronounced for announcers and anchors, who are expected to show a certain gravity, but it does exist. Income for both writers and actors tends to decrease with age. Even executives are often young these days. Age discrimination is not quite as prevalent in behind-the-scenes work, though older workers may find the hours and physical difficulties unpalatable.

Writers and other industry veterans counter that older workers are more skilled and experienced than younger ones. They argue that the only reason networks hire younger workers is that the networks have hired young executives in their effort to reach young viewers, and young executives do not want to work with older writers or performers. Whether the networks are correct about the business wisdom of these policies, they do make it harder for people to maintain careers in television throughout their lives. Some people working in the industry are trying to push back, to prove that older workers have the necessary talent to succeed and that older content can be popular across demographics, but it is difficult to fight against huge trends.

So what can you learn from this? Whatever your age, think and act like a young person. Keep up with new technology and popular culture. (Within reason, of course; do not make a fool of yourself trying to act too young.) Be flexible, be eager to please, and most of all, be energetic!

Producing, Directing, and Writing

There is no single path to producing or directing. Some people get there after years as a television writers. Others start out as actors, assistant directors, or production assistants. Some even come from the business side of television.

The most important qualities for producers and directors are experience, skill at handling people, grace under pressure, and raw talent. These qualities are more important than any formal training. Some successful producers and directors have college degrees in the field, but many do not. If you have the chance to study television production in college, it probably will not hurt your chances, but otherwise do not worry about that. It is better to gain experience in the television field by doing other jobs, such as finding a position as a production assistant.

Television Writing

Television writers are writers first and foremost. They need to know how to string words together. Reading a lot and practicing writing are the best way to build writing skills. Television writers should also watch a lot of television, not just for entertainment but to analyze the way a script is constructed. Most of all, a television writer needs a thick skin and a good deal of self-discipline. Short deadlines, regular rejection, and endless criticism are par for the course in this field.

Television writing jobs are at the production level. If you are new to the field, you should contact a production company to see what jobs are available. Many writers break in by becoming assistants to various production personnel. Finding a job as a production assistant, writers' assistant, or assistant to a producer can give you connections and help you learn the ropes, and can eventually lead to writing jobs. You could also find a job as a reader, reading and writing synopses of scripts for a network or a production company.

Spec Scripts

If you have experience writing and working for television, the best way to get hired is to write a really great spec script for a television series that already exists. The best spec scripts read as if they were actually written by a show's regular writers; they capture the characters and feel of the show exactly. If a show's producer likes your spec script, you may be called for an interview, which can lead to a position on the show's writing staff. The most successful writers churn out spec scripts every season so that their scripts reflect current seasons and situations. This maximizes their chances of selling a script, and is good practice besides.

Get an Agent

Any writer who is at the point of submitting spec scripts needs an agent. Agents can make a writer's job much easier. They have connections that writers do not necessarily have because they spend their days in meetings with various producers and network executives instead of sitting at their desks writing scripts. To get an agent, you need to submit a portfolio of your best work, including a résumé and at least one current spec script. Agents post listings on the Internet; search carefully to find the agents who represent the type of work you want to do. An agent's Web site should list some of the writers that the agent has represented and the shows on which they have worked. Expect to contact a number of agents before finding one to represent you.

Everyone Knows

Many television writers come to the field from copywriting in advertising agencies. Others start with jobs at educational film companies, corporate in-house film divisions, or government audiovisual departments. Writing these types of scripts can help you build your skills for television writing and provide you with a full-time paycheck at the same time.

Most television writers get hired during the annual staffing season from March through June. It is worth remembering that as a television writer, you will probably be self-employed. Working as a freelancer is inherently insecure. Freelancers must constantly be looking for their next job. People who succeed in television writing or any other kind of freelance writing come up with various strategies to keep themselves afloat. Some have spouses or domestic partners whose jobs provide benefits. Others take "real" jobs and write in their spare time.

Television writers who stick with the trade eventually build a reputation based on their stellar work and make enough connections in the field that they can actually make a good deal of money. If you hang in there, chances are good that you will get steady work and make a decent income. You may even work your way up to being a showrunner!

On the Screen

Though there are ways of advancing up the career ladder—by scoring bit parts in commercials or working as an extra, for instance—securing a job "in front of the camera" is a long-term process involving a great deal of patience, preparation, and natural ability. Still, those with resilience and a genuine love for the performing arts should not be dissuaded from exploring opportunities in this most demanding field.

Acting

Acting is one of the most competitive professions in the world. Lots and lots of people want to be actors. Only a small percentage of them become famous. Actors spend large amounts of time unemployed, or at least not employed as actors.

The first question to ask yourself if you think you want to act is whether or not you have any talent. Of course acting is a skill that can be taught, but it helps to begin with actual talent. Do you feel comfortable standing up in front of people and having them look at and listen to you? Can you speak clearly and naturally? Do you have good control over your physical movements? Can you "become" another person well enough to convince viewers that you are your character?

Actors spend their days with cameras pointing at them and hundreds of people scrutinizing and criticizing their faces, their bodies, their voices, and the way they speak. If you hate to be the center of attention, you will likely not succeed as an actor. If you cannot stand criticism, you should find another line of work right now.

You should also realize that appearance matters a great deal. That does not mean that only beautiful people can get acting jobs, though it certainly helps to be beautiful. It does mean, though, that acting jobs often go to people who look like the casting director's vision

Everyone
Knows

Work for Free!

If you can afford to work without pay for a little while, you will have both a better chance of landing a job in the first place and a better chance of working your way into a paid position down the line. Is the television studio willing to let you donate your time as a cable puller on a camera crew? Well, great! You are that much closer to a job as a camera operator. Has a studio executive offered you the opportunity to work for free making copies of scripts? This is your chance to read them.

Look upon this type of opportunity as a free education in the world of television. Lots of people pay for advanced training, so by that standard a volunteer position is a great deal! If you use your first job to learn everything you can and make as many connections as you can, you will find that donating your time is a worthwhile investment in your career.

of the characters needed. If you have the right look for a part your chances of getting it go up. (That being said, do pay attention to your appearance. Grooming and dress are extremely important in the world of performers.)

Acting Classes

Even the most naturally talented actors benefit from classes. Acting teachers can instruct you in voice projection, movement, expression, character, and all the other aspects of public performance. Proficient actors still participate in workshops and get coaching in order to improve their skills. Training can add a lot to your confidence, especially when you are put on the spot in an audition; if you are asked to read a scene you have never seen before or to improvise a scene with a stranger, experience and training can keep you from falling to pieces and ruining your chance.

There are acting classes available in most cities, especially New York and Los Angeles. You can take occasional classes while you do other types of work, or you can go all the way and earn a college degree in drama, acting, or similar field. Film school are a great place to get experience acting on camera, and they are also an excellent place to start networking.

Get an Agent

If you are serious about acting, you will need an agent. To get an agent you will need to make a portfolio that includes some headshots, a résumé, and a demo video of you acting. The format of this demo video will change with time. For years it was customary to submit a videotape. Nowadays you may submit a DVD or even a link to an online clip instead. Your prospective agent may post a list of requirements to guide you. You will probably have to approach many agents before you find one who will agree to represent you. Do not take this personally; agents see many portfolios from would-be actors but can only afford to represent a few. Once you have an agent, he or she will keep track of jobs that you could do and let you know about them.

Auditions, Casting Calls, and Screen Tests

No television producer will hire you without seeing you act, preferably on camera. Most shows choose performers through auditions and casting calls. Networks constantly issue notices for casting calls, inviting would-be performers to come and show themselves. Many casting calls occur in California and New York, often at network studios, though some shows do nationwide searches for talent. The casting call notice will tell you where to go and what time to show up.

Reality shows cast new performers constantly. Check out network Web sites to find out which shows are being cast and what you have to do to get into one. Reality show casting calls that require specific performers (e.g., the MTV show *Sixteen and Pregnant* needs performers with very specific qualifications) may provide would-be performers with an e-mail address at which they may contact the casting director.

There may be thousands of people at a casting call, all vying for the same few parts. To maximize your chances, you need to make yourself stand out in some way. Do your best to look like the character you want to play. Arrive on time, have your paperwork in order, and be patient and cooperative. Initially the casting director may just look at the people who have come to see who has the right

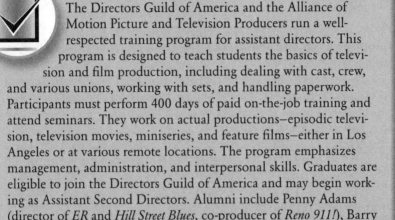

Best Practice

The Directors Guild of America and the Alliance of Motion Picture and Television Producers run a well-respected training program for assistant directors. This program is designed to teach students the basics of television and film production, including dealing with cast, crew, and various unions, working with sets, and handling paperwork. Participants must perform 400 days of paid on-the-job training and attend seminars. They work on actual productions—episodic television, television movies, miniseries, and feature films—either in Los Angeles or at various remote locations. The program emphasizes management, administration, and interpersonal skills. Graduates are eligible to join the Directors Guild of America and may begin working as Assistant Second Directors. Alumni include Penny Adams (director of *ER* and *Hill Street Blues*, co-producer of *Reno 911!*), Barry Thomas (first assistant director of *X Files*) and Bruce Cohen (producer of *Milk* and *American Beauty)*.

appearance. If your looks meet with approval, you may be asked to read some lines, perform a monologue, or act a scene with another performer. The director will see how you look and sound on camera. If the screen test goes well, you may be called back for another audition. It can sometimes take several auditions to land a part.

Remember, it is quite normal to attend many auditions before getting a part. If you are persistent, determined, and know the right people, you may eventually get cast in a show. Casting directors remember the faces they see regularly, so it pays to show up at as many casting calls as you can. Once you get your first television acting job, it will become easier to get your next one. Even a flop can build your résumé.

Extra Opportunities

Working as an extra is one way to break into television acting. Extras technically do not need any training and do not need to be as physically beautiful as actors. In fact, studios often want "normal-

INTERVIEW

The Chops for Props

Andrew M. Siegel
Property master

How long have you worked in television? What jobs have you had?
I've mostly worked in film for the last 20 years. I've been the assistant prop master on *Pee Wee's Playhouse*, *Dinosaurs*, and *The Office*.

How did you get into the field?
I answered an ad posted in the theater department at CSUN for an assistant art airector on a low budget film. I had been designing sets for theatrical productions and figured "Hey, how different could it be?"

What is your typical day like?
I've recently been the Prop Master on James Cameron's *Avatar*, and one of the Prop Masters on *GI Joe*. We typically get the props ready for the day's work, maintain the props and the prop continuity on the set, and try to get ready for the next day's work.

 The thing about props is that you have to be resourceful. I don't like to take "no" for an answer. If I have to stay on the phone to get you to find the thing that you want, I just stay on the phone until I

looking" people to fill in scenes as extras. Many people want to be extras, though, so it can still be challenging to find jobs. Most extras sign up with an extras casting service to help them find jobs. Some successful extras use agents. Many would-be extras take acting lessons to help them snag an agent. The best place to search for extra casting services and agents is the Internet. A quick Google search will turn up numerous possibilities. Do look through them carefully to ensure that you find a reputable service that will not simply take your money but not actually help you get ahead. As usual in the television field, connections can be very helpful in this area; talk to people you know who have used casting services or agents to find out whom they recommend.

get it. I ask if they know someone who has what I want, and usually they'll finally remember something. The hard ones to find are the ones you don't think are going to be hard. Every movie is different, which is what's cool about doing props. In one project it's all guns and knives, and the next it's all pens and briefcases. But if you care about it, you want to find the perfect pen of the perfect briefcase. Then conversely the hard part is that sometimes you just don't have the time and you're not going to get that—you just get what you get on the day, and that can be frustrating.

What tips would you give to someone who is just starting out in the television industry?
You just have to meet a lot of people. That's really the key—the more people you know, the more opportunities you have to prove to one of them that you can really be good at something. This thing about this business is that jobs are relatively short, so you come in and then you're done, which is kind of cool. But you meet someone and maybe you can go on with them to do something. You just have to be a good networker. If it's convenient for them to remember you they will, but there are a lot people who are vying for every job, and sometimes it's just a matter of being in the right place at the right time, or calling the person you need to call right away.

For a while I did a bunch of commercials. I was on *Avatar* for 14 months the first time and six months the next. Anyone I was doing commercials with forgot about me. It's hard to keep the relationships open.

Reality Shows and Game Shows

Over the past decade reality shows have launched a number of celebrity careers. Some examples include *American Idol* alums Carrie Underwood and Chris Daughtry, *Queer Eye*'s Ted Allen and Carson Kressley, and *Project Runway*'s Jay McCarroll. If you want to be on television but do not like the idea of acting, this approach may be for you. There are now a large number of reality shows on television, and many of them regularly hold casting calls for future performers. If you meet the criteria of a particular show, you may find yourself an overnight celebrity.

Reality show casting calls take place all over the country, usually in major cities. Producers are looking for people who will perform well on camera and who are willing to expose their "real" selves to the world. Most reality shows have prospective performers fill out an application explaining why they would be good for the show and perhaps submit short films of themselves. In some cases, such as *American Idol*, producers are looking for actual talent. In others, they are looking for just the opposite, people who are in desperate need of help but who have the potential to look or sound good after the show's intervention.

Game shows do not tend to generate as many celebrities as reality shows, but there are also many more opportunities available for people who would like to appear. Game shows also use an application process to pick contestants. The game show *Jeopardy*, for example, holds regular auditions in Los Angeles and in some other cities, at which participants take a written test and then, if they pass, play a mock game of *Jeopardy*. Successful applicants may be called to appear on the show. Every show's Web site explains how to become a contestant. If you want a career on the screen, there are worse ways to get exposure than doing well on a game show, and if you win, the money cannot hurt.

Announcers and Anchors

Producers of news and informational programs are looking for different qualities in their on-screen performers than producers of dramas or comedies. First, they are looking for people who have a nice appearance, who speak clearly and enunciate well, and who can read scripts without messing up. Second, they are looking for people who are intelligent, well-educated, familiar with current events, and who can talk easily with strangers. They want announcers who can think on their feet and who can respond to sudden changes of plan without losing the beat.

To become a television reporter, you will probably need a college degree in journalism, broadcasting, communications studies, or a similar program that teaches you how to gather information and put together stories. Some specialized reporters have degrees in fields such as meteorology, economics, law, or political science. You will certainly need to be able to speak clearly without a script while a camera points at your face. Some knowledge of camera and sound operation is also helpful because television reporters often complete their stories in the field with only one or two technicians.

Many television reporters have broken into the field by working for free as interns at television stations. There is some overlap between print and television journalism; you may be able to use print journalism experience to get a job in television. To succeed as a television journalist, you must be persistent. This job requires many hours of work, and only the most dedicated stick it out for many years. If you want to move up to announcing from a desk in the studio, you will first need to do a good job as a reporter. You may need to bring yourself to the attention of the news director, perhaps volunteering to take on tough jobs and going the extra mile on your assignments. It helps to be willing to work undesirable hours. If you have good ideas for shows and stories, share them, and offer to produce them yourself.

In order to advance in this field, you will probably have to move occasionally. Reporters often switch stations as they move up in the field. You may start out working at a small local station, and then advance to a higher-profile job in a bigger city before reaching the news desk at CNN. Most announcers and anchors get their jobs by sending samples of their on-air work to stations. As with all television jobs, networking is crucial.

Behind the Scenes

If you are interested in working on the technical side of television, you will need to both learn the technical skills involved in doing your job and the ins and outs of finding jobs and working with a crew.

Get Some Training

Many technicians, makeup people, and other behind the scenes professionals have some academic training in their fields. Technical high schools and colleges offer courses in video production, computer graphics, film editing, cosmetology, hair styling, and other useful topics. Some professionals earn bachelor's or graduate degrees in their specialties from colleges or universities with film and television programs. These programs often run their own television stations to give students real-life practice in all aspects of television production.

Do you really need to go to school? That depends on your specialty. If you go into a field such as computer graphics, you may need a good deal of training. Camera operators, on the other hand, can sometimes enter the field with just a high school diploma. In many cases experience is more important than academic credentials. If you want a job behind the camera, get some practice shooting footage. You may be able to find a job with a video company, such as a company that shoots videos of weddings, and gain some experience that you can later parlay into a job at a television studio. If you want to work as a makeup artist you may need to get a degree in cosmetology, but the practical experience you get once you start working as a makeup assistant will probably be more significant to your overall career success. Wardrobe people may just spend years working in

Fast Facts

Some writers get started by attending writer training programs. Warner Brothers, Disney, Nickelodeon, the Writers' Guild, and many other organizations offer programs. Most of these programs are in California, and require participants to attend classes in person, which makes housing and transportation a real consideration. NBC Universal, for example, offers a program called Writers on the Verge, which is a 10-week program designed to polish writers' skills to prepare them for staff writer positions (positions on NBC shows are a possibility, but not guaranteed). The program takes students through the process of creating a spec script and pitching it to a network. This program is not for beginners, but for writers who are nearly ready to start working. To apply, you have to submit a spec script for a show that aired new episodes in the previous year, along with an essay explaining why you want to work as a television writer and what makes you a good investment. The competition to get into this program and similar ones is fierce; make sure your application is the best you can possibly produce.

the wardrobe department, learning their job as they go.

One great way to gain experience and make connections at the same time is to do an internship with a television station or network. Interns get to help shoot and edit field productions, operate cameras and sound boards in studios, work in the office, and maybe produce their own content such as public service announcements for local nonprofits. Studios and networks typically want their interns to have taken at least basic courses in television production. There are hundreds of internships available around the country, both at small local stations and at television networks in big cities. An Internet search can turn up possibilities in your area. High school and college career offices or communications faculty may be able to help you find an internship.

Start Out Small

Almost every successful television technician starts out in an entry-level job such as production assistant or cable puller. Some established professionals suggest that if operating a camera is your ultimate goal, working as a cable puller is better than taking a job as a production assistant because a cable puller works directly with the camera operator whereas a production assistant may do odd jobs for everyone. On the other hand, if you are offered a PA position on a really good show, taking it could further your career more than doing grunt work on a mediocre program simply because it will provide you with better connections and networking opportunities. Whatever entry-level job you take, make it your business to watch the camera operators and offer to help them when you can.

Once you get into the field, your body of work becomes more important than your background. If you are a camera operator or editor, producers will want to see what you have done. They will want to see how you frame shots or cut scenes, and whether you have creativity and a good eye. Makeup artists and hair stylists can show their work with photographs and video clips.

Your early jobs are your opportunity to impress your bosses and colleagues with your skill and professionalism. Technical people must be ready to do jobs at a moment's notice. If you do hair or makeup, you may need to touch up performers during short breaks. Be prepared for these moments; have whatever tools you need at the ready. If you are working as a VT operator, you need to have

INTERVIEW

Getting Ahead Slowly

Melissa Harrison
Art department coordinator, *The Office*

How did you get into the field?

I moved to Los Angeles and went to USC, but it wasn't the degree that got me jobs. In fact, USC didn't really do much job placement at all—it was really up to us all after we graduated to just pound the pavement for gigs until we scrounged something up. It was quite difficult at first. I went for about six months without any job at all, but I just kept pounding away till one shook loose. An important part of the job hunt is not being afraid to sound like a fool, and not standing on your pride. Sometimes you just have to cold-call a company and ask, "Hi, my name is ____, and I'm looking for a new show to work on. Could you use a PA on your show?"

I know plenty of people who graduated and then could not humble themselves to work as a "lowly" PA. That's really the wrong mindset—when you start in this business, you really are nobody. No matter how great you were in college, you've got to pay your dues and start at the bottom in order to work your way up into a better job. And for people who work hard and do good work, they won't be stuck being a PA for very long. The ability to advance will quickly present itself.

your clips ready to go at the precise moment they are called for. Unfortunately, mistakes in this area are much more noticeable than days and weeks of good work; you do not want to be "discovered" as the production assistant who accidentally unplugged the camera or something equally unfortunate.

The Joys of Intermittent Employment

Television work can be sporadic and unpredictable. (If you want a steady nine-to-five job, you should consider a different field of employment!) You will maximize your chances of success if you are

What tips would you give to someone contemplating a career in television?
Don't come into the business with a big ego. There are a million egos in Los Angeles, and strutting around like you're something important isn't going to endear you to your boss.

Don't be discouraged if you wind up working a few jobs you don't like. That's one of the beautiful things about being on shows. They don't last very long! If you don't enjoy one, you'll probably be done with it in under one year's time.

Don't expect it to be all fun and games. Do expect 12-hour days. Minimum. Set days are 12 hours, standard. It's not unusual for days to go into 16 or 18 hours.

Be sure to know your rights when you work. If you don't, you'll be exploited. Know when overtime pay starts. Know that you're required by law to be given breaks. Don't let the pressure of working on set trick you into doing stupid, risky things like driving after being awake for 24 hours, or handling equipment you don't feel safe handling.

Take the time to be polite and genuinely kind to everyone that you can. Especially including the PAs and security guards. It's these "low on the totem pole" folks that do 75 percent of the grunt work on sets, and having them as your friends can really be mutually beneficial.

Get to work 15 minutes ahead of your call-time. Do not ever, ever, *ever* be late. Being on time is one of the easiest things you can do, but one of the most damaging if you fail at it. Your boss doesn't care that you're tired—he or she is way more tired and stressed out than you are, and still manages to show up on time. I've seen multiple people who in other respects were fine at their jobs fired for being late.

completely flexible and available to work at a moment's notice. You may need to find another source of income during downtime, but your television career will benefit if you can drop everything and take assignments when they appear.

You may get a regular job with a salary and benefits; they do exist, especially in broadcasting. Even in that case, your hours may be very irregular. This can be both a benefit and a burden. Odd hours do allow for flexibility, which can be desirable. On the other hand, if you have a family and regular responsibilities, it can be very difficult to make those mesh with an insane television schedule. Child care can be hard to arrange late at night, early in the morning, or all weekend long.

Many television production jobs are freelance. That means that if you take a job, you will be considered an independent contractor, not an employee. There is a world of difference between those two terms. An independent contractor is a person who does a job for another but does not enter into an employee–employer relationship. An independent contractor does not receive regular compensation or benefits from the employer, and is usually free to work for others simultaneously. An employee is more under the control of the employer, and receives a regular wage or salary. Employees generally receive more benefits, such as health insurance.

Getting health insurance and saving for retirement can be big challenges for people who work in the television industry. If you find a full-time position with a television company, your employer may provide health insurance for you, but many television workers are not able to do this. Individual health insurance plans are notoriously expensive and cover very little.

The self-employed can try various strategies to procure coverage for themselves and their families. If you have a spouse or domestic partner with a more "normal" full-time job, you can probably be covered by his or her health plan, usually for an additional fee. Many universities have insurance pools for their alumni. Unions offer health and retirement plans to members.

Hours and Overtime

If you are paid by the hour, you are probably eligible for overtime pay. Overtime generally begins after you have worked 40 hours in a week, and is usually paid at one-and-a-half times the regular hourly rate. You may also be eligible for other types of premium pay, which is pay for work outside normal working hours. Some employers pay double for work done after you have worked 80 hours in a week—the money can really add up, but those weeks are hard! Be sure you find out how your pay rates work. If you sign a contract, read it carefully, and ask questions about anything confusing.

Retirement

If you remain self-employed for most of your working career, you and you alone will be responsible for supporting yourself in retirement. Though retirement planning may seem the least of your worries, it is a very good idea to take some action while you are still young. Do not rely on Social Security alone to take care of you in your old age!

There are several good retirement planning options for the self-employed. An individual retirement account, or IRA, allows you to save money for retirement with some tax advantages. Contributions to a traditional IRA are tax-deductible in the year that you make them, but earnings on the IRA are taxable. Contributions to a Roth IRA are taxed in the year that you make them, but then they grow tax-free thereafter. You can only deposit $5,000 a year into a traditional IRA or Roth IRA. A SEP IRA allows you to deposit about 20 percent of your earnings into an IRA, up to a fairly high limit, which makes it a very good option. A Keogh plan is similar to a corporate profit-sharing plan or a defined benefit pension plan. You can also open a solo 401(k), which is similar to an employer's 401(k). You can maintain some or all of these retirement accounts even if you have an employer-sponsored retirement plan for some of your career.

Remember, interest compounds. The younger you start saving for retirement, the less you will have to save every year to make your goal. Even small contributions early in your career will add up over your lifetime.

Taxes

When you get paid for your work in television, be sure you know whether your employer is withholding taxes for you. If not, you will have to pay those taxes yourself. The self-employed must estimate their tax burden for the year and pay those taxes to the I.R.S. every quarter. They must also pay the self-employment tax, which is the portion of Social Security and Medicare normally paid by employers. This tax will take an extra 15 percent of your earnings, but half of it is deductible.

Most television employees, like most workers in the United States, are considered "at-will" employees. That means they are hired without a contract. An employer can fire an at-will employee at any time for any or no reason. Likewise, the employee can quit at any time. The exception to this is employment governed by an employment contract, which is a contract that specifies the terms of employment: the employment period, duties, compensation, and any acceptable reasons for ending the contract early. Contracts are fairly common in the television world, but they tend to be short-term, as in several weeks. (The WGA, for example, requires employers to give staff writers week-to-week contracts that guarantee work for between six and 40 weeks.) If you are offered an employment contract, read the terms very carefully. Be sure you understand the contract before you sign it!

Non-Compete Agreements

Some television broadcast companies impose non-compete clauses on employees. A non-compete requires an ex-employee to avoid competing with his or her former employer for a set period of time. This is particularly common with news anchors, announcers and other employees who appear on-camera; a non-compete agreement may state that if an employee leaves his or her job and goes to work for a competing station in the same geographical area, that employee may not appear on the air for several months or years. Television stations use these agreements to prevent "star" employees from leaving for local competitors; stations invest a great deal of money in developing their talent, and fear that long-time employees will take away company secrets with them. Employees, however, hate the restriction on their mobility. A number of states have banned non-compete agreements because they prevent people from working continuously.

Talk Like a Pro

401(k) A defined contribution plan run by a company that allows employees to save or invest part of their pre-tax salary in a retirement account.

accommodation Meeting someone's needs or demands; arranging a job so that it is possible for someone to perform it, such as adjusting a schedule or work methods to make it possible for a disabled person to perform it.

ADA Americans with Disabilities Act, a federal statute prohibiting discrimination against disabled people in jobs, transportation, and services.

ADEA Age Discrimination in Employment Act of 1967, a federal statute prohibiting employment discrimination on the basis of age; it protects people age 40 and older.

affirmative action plan (AAP) A plan intended to correct employment discrimination by making an effort to recruit and hire people who come from underrepresented categories, such as women or minorities, and hiring them when they are as qualified as other applicants who are more typical of previous hires.

agent A person who represents an actor, writer, or director, handling business negotiations in return for a portion of the client's earnings.

air time Time on screen, on the air.

animation The process of creating a film by drawing or using a computer to render individual frames that, when run together, form a moving picture. Cartoons are a type of animation.

aperture A measurement of the width of the opening allowing light to enter a camera, also known as f-stop. A wide aperture is a large opening that lets in a lot of light, allowing filming in low light, but has a shallow depth of field; in other words, the objects focused on will be clear but everything in front of and behind them will be blurry. A narrow aperture allows less light to enter but can create more depth of field, i.e. a much longer range of objects in focus.

art department The department of a production in charge of the visual appearance of the production, under the supervision of the art director or production designer.

aspect ratio The proportions of a screen; the ration of height to width.

at-will Describes an employee hired without a contract of employment, meaning that either the employer or the employee can terminate the employment at any time for any reason; employment is entirely voluntarily for both parties and exists only for an indefinite period.

audition A process in which a performer attempts to win a part in a television show or other production by doing a short performance for the director or casting director.

automated dialogue replacement (ADR) The recording of dialogue during postproduction, done by having actors read their lines timed to coincide with filmed footage. ADR can be used to record a soundtrack in a different language from the original or to correct poorly recorded dialogue. Also called looping.

axis of action An imaginary line between the two main actors in a scene that divides the screen into right and left portions.

background artist The person who designs the art at the back of a set that serves as a background for shots. In animation, the person who designs the background on which the action takes place.

backlot An area on a studio's property with no buildings or other structures, used to film open-air and wilderness scenes.

best boy The assistant to a chief lighting technician or gaffer.

billing The relative placement and size of names in the opening credits and publicity materials for a film or television show. A production's star will have his or her name listed first and/or largest; this is "top billing."

bit part A tiny part in a television show that has at least one spoken line but not very many; in British television, for example, an actor with a bit part has fewer than six spoken lines.

black and white Shot in only black and white, with no colors; the first television programs were all black and white.

blacklisting The practice of placing an actor, writer, director, or other film or television professional on a "blacklist" of individuals who should not be hired because of their participation in unsavory political activities; this was done regularly during the 1950s, when Senator McCarthy tried to root Communists out of the entertainment industry. Unions sometimes still blacklist people for engaging in anti-union activity.

blocking A director's plan for actors' movement throughout a scene.

blooper A mistake made during filming, such as an actor saying the wrong word. Bloopers are sometimes humorous.

bluescreen A blank background in front of which actors perform scenes that have backgrounds added later, perhaps with computer-generated images.

body double An actor whose body is used to replace that of the main actor, either because the main actor's body does not have the correct look (e.g., physical fitness) or because the main actor does not want to appear nude on screen.

boom microphone A microphone on a long pole, or boom, that can be moved around to capture sounds.

boom operator A technician on the sound crew who holds a boom microphone.

bounce board A large white board used by the camera or lighting crew to reflect light onto a scene.

breakdown script A list, often assembled by the continuity department, of all props, people, equipment, and other items needed for each day of shooting.

call An order to appear at a shoot at a certain day and time.

call sheet A list of which actors are called for which scenes.

cameo A short appearance onscreen by a famous actor who is not a regular member of a show's cast.

camera crew The group of technicians in charge of setting up and operating the cameras for a production.

Problem
Solving

What does a production company do when an actor is supposed to appear in a dangerous situation or when a character is supposed to be heavily muscled and the actor portraying him is not? It uses a double, of course.

A double is an actor who takes the place of a main actor in certain scenes for various reasons. A stunt double may appear in dangerous scenes, while a body double may stand in for an actor when nudity is called for (or if the titled actor's body just is not up to close-up scrutiny).

Doubles are not the same as stand-ins, who solve an entirely different problem. Setting up a shot can be a time-consuming process, and it is usually necessary to have people actually standing on the set where the actors belong. No producer, though, wants to exhaust a performer by making him or her stand under the lights for hours on end while no shooting is taking place. A stand-in stands in an actor's place on the set while the camera and lighting crews set levels and then steps aside for the actor when the shot begins. A stand-in usually needs to be about the same size as the actor and have the same coloring so that the levels will be accurate.

cast The actors who appear in a television, film, or theatrical production. The act of choosing an actor for a part in a production.

casting agency A business that works to match talent, i.e. actors and performers, with jobs, and to help production companies and networks find talent.

casting call An announcement that a television production will be looking for performers at a specific place, date, and time, inviting anyone who wants to audition for the part to appear.

caterer The company that provides meals on set for cast and crew.

cattle call A mass audition in which a large number of performers all hoping for the same part or parts present themselves to the casting director. All the aspiring performers are kept together in one place like a herd of cattle. Usually only performers without agents come to cattle calls.

CCU Camera control unit, a device used to control the technical settings of a video camera remotely from a control room and providing an interface between the camera and a vision mixer.

censorship Removing scenes or words from a show in order to keep it from violating certain standards of decency.

CGI Computer generated imagery, computer graphics that create special effects. Much animation today is done with CGI.

character actor An actor who specializes in performing a certain type of characters, who is usually cast in supporting roles.

choreographer A person who creates dance sequences and teaches them to performers.

chroma key A method of removing the color from one image and overlaying another image in its place in order to create a composite image. This technique is used with a bluescreen or greenscreen to allow the studio to shoot footage of a performer without having the entire scene in place. It is commonly used in weather broadcasts.

chyron Lower third; graphics placed in the bottom of the screen, such as the identity of the person speaking.

cinematography The art of capturing moving images on camera.

clapper A board with a movable top edge used to synchronize picture and sound at the start of a take; on it are written the name of the show, scene and take number, and date and time. The person who claps the clapper is called a clapper-loader.

claymation A type of animation in which the characters are made of clay or some similar moldable substance and are subtly changed from shot to shot to create the appearance of movement.

clean take A take in which no errors occur.

cliffhanger An end to a scene or program that occurs at a moment of high dramatic tension that is left unresolved in order to get viewers to watch the next installment of the show.

closed captioning The practice of displaying a transcript of the dialogue and sound on screen for the benefit of those who cannot hear the television's sound.

COBRA Consolidated Omnibus Budget Reconciliation Act of 1986, a law passed by Congress that requires insurers to continue group coverage for individuals who would otherwise lose their health coverage due to ending their employment. COBRA coverage applies to people who worked for employers with at least 20 employees with group health coverage. Under COBRA, the former employee is allowed to pay his or her own premiums to continue the group coverage for 18 months after leaving employment.

colorist A person who adjusts the color and lighting of the scenes of a television show after it has been shot and edited.

color temperature The temperature of a given color of light; blue light has a higher color temperature than yellow.

color timing The process of matching colors in scenes from shot to shot.

colorization A process used to convert black and white programs to color.

commercial A short film that attempts to convince viewers to purchase a particular product; a television advertisement.

Communications Act of 1934 The federal law that created the FCC and that regulated television broadcasting for much of the 20th century; partially replaced by the Telecommunications Act of 1996.

compensatory (comp) time Vacation time offered to employees instead of extra pay for work done beyond the normal amount expected.

composite To combine different images into one scene, such as adding a background to the area where a scene was shot in front of a bluescreen.

continuity A movie's consistency from scene to scene; i.e., the degree to which each scene has all the components it is meant to have, including actors, costumes, props, and hair styles.

costume The clothing and accessories worn by an actor or performer.

costumer A person who handles the costumes worn by actors.

crane shot A shot taken by a camera mounted on a crane so that it can move smoothly above the action.

cutting room floor In the days of film, the floor of the room in which the editor worked; any film the editor removed ended up on the cutting room floor, never to be seen by viewers.

creator The person primarily responsible for the creation of a show; often the showrunner or head writer.

crew The people who work on a television show behind the scenes.

cut To end a shot; to change camera angle within a scene.

daytime drama A dramatic program aired during daytime hours; a soap opera.

Department of Labor A branch of the federal government that protects workers and retirees by administering labor laws that guarantee rights to safe employment, minimum wages and overtime, freedom from discrimination, unemployment insurance, and retirement and health care benefits. The DOL also tracks national economic trends, supports collective bargaining, and helps employers and workers find one another.

depth of field The range of distance at which a camera's shot is in focus.

develop To work on a script and concept for a television program in order to persuade a network to produce it.

dialogue Words spoken by actors.

director The person in charge of telling the actors what to do on camera; the person in charge of shooting a program.

discrimination Unequal or unfair treatment of people based on categories such as race, sex, religion, or age.

dissolve To fade out one shot while replacing it with another.

documentary A film that tells a true story or attempts to inform viewers about a topic through the use of interviews, live footage, computer animation, voice-over, and other techniques.

Everyone Knows

Throughout the entertainment industry, you will hear the term "talent." This term refers to the people who appear on screen or on stage, the actors and performers. They are called the talent regardless of whether they actually have talent, but one assumes they do.

dolly A wheeled cart used to move a camera along a track. The person who moves the dolly is known as a dolly grip.

dope sheet A list of scenes already filmed. Also used as a storyboard in the production of animated films.

dresser A crew member who helps performers dress in their costumes.

dubbing *See* automated dialogue replacement.

DVR Digital video recorder, a device used to record television programs in digital format.

edit To rearrange shots so that they appear in the desired order.

employee A person hired by another to do a particular job in exchange for pay. An employee is usually under the employer's control, as opposed to an independent contractor, who is not, and the employer can dictate the methods an employee uses to accomplish tasks.

employment contract A contract that specifies terms of employment, such as employment period, duties, compensation, and reasons for terminating the contract.

episode One program of a television series.

exempt Not eligible for overtime under the FLSA (Fair Labor Standards Act); professional, administrative, and executive workers, employees who work in outside sales, and employees in particular computer-related jobs are usually exempt.In order for a worker to be classified as exempt, he she must be paid a salary and not an hourly wage, that salary must be at least a certain minimum amount, and he or she must perform duties that are primarily administrative, professional, or executive.

exposition Background scenes used to establish the setting of a story.

exterior A scene that takes place outside.

extra An actor who appears in a scene without speaking, mainly to give the scene the right atmosphere.

fade To transition smoothly from a scene to black.

FCC Federal Communications Commission, the federal agency that regulates broadcasting by television, radio, telephone, satellite, etc.

flashback A scene that depicts action that occurred before the time of the main action of the show.

FLSA Fair Labor Standards Act, a federal statute passed in 1938 that set a minimum wage, a maximum work week, overtime rule, child labor regulations, and established categories of employees who receive different kinds of pay and work on different kinds of schedules. The FLSA has been revised several times since it was written to reflect changes in work categories and amounts of pay.

FMLA Family and Medical Leave Act, a federal law enacted in 1993 that guarantees workers unpaid leave to take care of their children or family members or for their own health problems; the FMLA applies to employers with at least 50 employees and usually guarantees 12 weeks of leave per year.

focus To adjust a camera to make the image sharp; the sharpness of an image.

focus group A group of people brought in to watch a television program and give their reactions to it; often used by market research analysts to determine the likely success of a show.

freelance Self-employed; working on a project basis rather than as a permanent employee of a company.

FSA Flexible spending account, an account that allows an employee to save pre-tax dollars to cover specific eligible expenses, such as health care or dependent care.

gaffer The head of the lighting department, or chief electrician.

greenscreen A green background used as a background for shooting when intending to add a different background to the final scene; the greenscreen is replacing the bluescreen because it is easier to separate green than blue from other colors.

grip A lighting technician.

head shot A close-up photograph of an actor's or performer's face, neck, and shoulders, included in the performer's portfolio to show what the performer looks like. Head shots are usually done in a glamorous style by a professional photographer with professionally done hair and makeup.

HIPAA The Health Insurance Portability and Accountability Act of 1996, a law that protects the health insurance coverage of workers who change or lose jobs by allowing those workers to purchase coverage within a specified period, and preventing insurers from excluding certain pre-existing conditions from new coverage or from denying coverage to people with certain health conditions or charging them more for coverage. It also protects the privacy of workers by insisting that patient records remain confidential.

host The person who runs a show on screen, introducing the show and guests and conducting interviews.

indecency Content that is considered inappropriate for a general audience because it uses profane words or is sexual in nature.

independent contractor A person who does a job for another but does not enter into an employee-employer relationship; the independent contractor uses his or her own methods, does the job on his or her own schedule, is not under the control of the employer as to how the job is accomplished, does not receive regular compensation or benefits from the employer, and is usually free to work for others simultaneously.

infomercial A television program that functions as an extended advertisement for a product, mainly by attempting to educate viewers about the product and the reasons for using it.

interior A scene that takes place inside a building.

IRA Individual retirement account, a tax-favored savings plan used to accumulate money for retirement.

Keogh plan A retirement plan that allows self-employed people to save pre-tax income for retirement, similar to a 401K.

key grip A chief lighting technician.

layoff Termination of an employee for economic reasons that result in his or her job being eliminated, as opposed to firing the employee for some cause such as incompetence.

layout Blocking; the movement of actors and camera angles within a scene.

lead An actor with one of the main parts in a show. Often a show will have a male lead and a female lead.

light board Console that can be used to adjust the combination of lights that are on and their respective levels.

lighting The lights used to illuminate the scenes in a show, often provided by artificial lights.

lighting department The section of the crew in charge of lighting.

lined script A copy of the shooting script used to record what portions of scenes have been shot.

line producer A producer who is in charge of managing the details of a shoot; also called a unit production manager.

live area The portion of the set that is visible on camera.

local affiliate A television station that broadcasts a network's programming to the station's local area.

location Filming outdoors in real settings as opposed to in a studio.

location manager The person who arranges for filming to take place in various locations.

location scout A person who searches for good locations for filming.

lower third Graphics or text placed in the bottom of the screen, such as the name and title of the person speaking in the scene.

lyrics The words to a song.

makeup Cosmetics applied to performers to enhance their appearance or achieve an artistic effect, such as making a young performer appear to be much older.

mise-en-scène The totality of a scene, including all the artistic elements that go into creating it.

Fast Facts

A miniseries, or mini-series, is a television production that tells a complete story in multiple episodes, usually aired over the course of several days. They are often adaptations of popular works of literature. Though experts disagree on how many episodes it takes to make a miniseries, generally they run between three and twelve episodes. Miniseries were extremely popular in the 1970s and 1980s. The biggest miniseries all featured big-name casts and multi-generational family sagas, preferably with a great deal of romance and tragedy, sprawling settings, and huge budgets. The first major miniseries was *Rich Man, Poor Man*, a 1976 adaptation of Irwin Shaw's novel. *Roots*, the 1977 miniseries based on Alex Haley's book tracing the history of his ancestors in the American South, was the first miniseries blockbuster, attracting some 130 million viewers, making it the highest-rated program of its time. The 1983 miniseries *The Thorn Birds*, based on the novel by Colleen McCullogh, attracted nearly as many viewers as *Roots*, despite (or perhaps because of) its controversial subject matter, a Roman Catholic priest's illicit relationship with a woman. After the 1980s miniseries became less popular, perhaps because cable and satellite television provided so many more viewing options than the three networks had in earlier years.

mixing console A device used to select, adjust, and combine several different sources of sound. Also called an audio mixer or sound board.

montage A series of images spliced together to create a feeling or tell a short story.

motion capture A technique of creating computer animation by digitally capturing the actions of a live actor or moving object.

music supervisor The person who chooses and coordinates the music used in a show in collaboration with composers and music editors.

Nielsen ratings Relative ranking of popularity of television programs compiled by Nielsen media, used by advertisers to determine which shows will generate viewers for their commercials and by networks to decide which shows to keep on the air and which to cancel.

network A company that distributes broadcast content to television stations.

non-compete An agreement signed by an employee in which the employee promises not to work for the employer's direct competitor for a specified period of time after leaving the current employer, designed to prevent the employee from bringing to the competitor any trade secrets he or she learned while working for the current employer.

obscenity Words or images that offend general standards of sexual morality.

off-book The state of an actor who has memorized his or her lines and no longer needs a script.

outtake A take of a scene that is not usable in the final production due to errors committed during filming. Outtakes, or bloopers, are sometimes compiled into collections and shown as humorous films.

overtime Extra pay for work done beyond forty hours in a week, usually at one and a half times the worker's usually hourly rate.

paid leave Time off during which the employee is paid his or her usual compensation.

pan To move a camera from right to left or left to right, creating a sweeping shot.

pan and scan A technique of adapting a movie for television that involves chopping off portions of the side of the movie in order to fit the narrower aspect ratio of a television screen.

pixelate To digitally blur a portion of an image in order to make it impossible to see it clearly. This is typically done to obscure the faces of people who do not wish to reveal their identities or to cover genitalia.

point of view (POV) A camera shot taken from a character's position, revealing what that character sees.

pornography A film or video made solely to depict graphic sex for the purpose of titillating the audience.

postproduction The work done on a television program after shooting is complete, including editing, visual effects, CGI, and dubbing.

premium pay Extra pay given to employees who work at unusual times, such as Sunday, holidays, or at night, or for overtime or standby work; premium pay rates can vary depending on the reason for the extra pay. Overtime pay is a type of premium pay.

premium television Subscription-based television often broadcast without commercials.

prime time The evening hours in which the largest number of viewers is watching television, generally 7 A.M. to 10 A.M. or 8 P.M. to 11 P.M.

production The period in which a show is being shot.

production assistant A low-level employee who does various odd jobs on the set. Many television professionals start out as production assistants and use the experience and connections to work their way into better jobs.

profanity Bad language; language that is vulgar, rude, and socially unacceptable, particularly so-called curse words.

prop Any item that appears on a set and that can be picked up, touched, or used by an actor.

props master The person in charge of acquiring props, setting them up for shots, and taking care of them.

prosthetic A device or object attached to an actor's face or body in order to give him or her the required appearance; for example, sometimes an actor's nose is enlarged with a prosthetic nose.

publicist A person who works to create publicity for an actor, television show, or other public entity. A publicist is usually paid a regular fee, unlike an agent, who takes a percentage of the client's earnings.

puppeteer A person who designs, builds, and manipulates puppets. The Muppets were manipulated by puppeteers.

pyrotechnics Explosions and fires deliberately set by a technician as part of the setting for a show.

reasonable accommodation A change to the workplace that can allow a disabled person to work there, such as modifying furniture, or changing schedules or instructions, required by the Rehabilitation Act of 1973; an employer is required to make reasonable accommodations to allow disabled employees to work unless such accommodation would cause undue hardship to the employer.

rerun A showing of an episode of a television program subsequent to its initial appearance; a repeat showing of an old program.

safe area An area outside of the camera's viewfinder that will not be seen on camera; *see* live area.

safe harbor The hours between prime time and morning programming (i.e., 10 P.M. to 6 A.M.) in which networks and stations are free to broadcast content that does not adhere to the profanity rules that apply during more popular viewing times.

salary A regular fixed payment made by an employer to an employee for work performed, usually set by the year and paid once or twice a month, regardless of the hours worked by the employee.

scene A portion of a program all of which takes place in the same place at about the same time.

score The soundtrack of a film or television program.

screen test An audition in which an actor performs a monologue or scene on camera, allowing the casting director or director to see what that person would look like on a television screen.

script The written document that encapsulates a television program, describing setting, characters, actions, and providing dialogue.

SEP IRA An individual retirement account that allows a self-employed individual to save up to 20 percent of yearly income tax-free.

serial A continuing story that is broadcast in portions each day or week. Most soap operas are serials.

series A television show with multiple episodes that use recurring characters and story lines but that does not necessarily tell a continuous story.

set The physical environment in which action is filmed.

sexual harassment Employment discrimination that involves sexual demands and acts, involving perpetrators and victims of either sex.

sitcom Situation comedy; a comedy that takes place mostly in a single setting with the same broadly drawn characters.

shoot To film a scene.

shooting script The script used during shooting of a program to guide shooting.

shot A chunk of continuous footage taken by one camera of a single scene.

showrunner The head writer or executive producer of a program; the person who is responsible for the show's concept and its creation.

sketch A short skit or scene often used in comedy shows such as *Saturday Night Live*.

soap opera A drama that depicts a continuing story over the course of days and weeks, usually romantic and melodramatic, aimed primarily at a female audience watching television during the day.

speaking role A role in which an actor speaks on camera.

spec script A script for an existing show that a writer creates without an assignment in the hopes of getting a job on the show or selling the script.

stand-in A person with looks similar to a lead actor who takes that actor's place in scenes during set-up.

station A company that broadcasts television programs to a local area. A station may broadcast content from a network or locally produced content.

steadicam A camera mounted on a support that isolates the operator's movements from the camera's, preventing the operator's movements from causing shaky or jumpy shots.

stock footage Film in a studio's archives that is used to fill in spaces in a show.

studio A company that produces films and television programs; a building or room in which television programs are shot.

supporting actor An actor who performs a role that is important but less significant than a lead.

sweeps One of several month-long periods during the year in which the ratings are compiled for television programs. Television networks and stations make a particular effort to broadcast popular content to attract viewers during sweeps periods.

syndication The sale of the broadcast rights to television shows to multiple stations.

take A single recording of a scene.

timeshifting Using technology such as a DVR to watch content on one's own schedule, separate from the network's broadcasting schedule, and to customize the content by fast-forwarding, rewinding, pausing, or skipping portions.

trade secret A formula, process, machine, plan, method of compiling information, or other form of information that is known to and used exclusively by a single business that keeps it secret from competitors because the knowledge gives the business an advantage and allowing the secret out could give competitors an advantage instead.

type A person's look or general appearance.

typecasting The identification of particular actors with particular roles.

unemployment insurance Insurance provided by the federal and state governments to protect workers who become unemployed through no fault of their own, such as workers who are laid off.

upfront An industry event at which networks show their new season's programs to advertisers, and the advertisers buy commercial time. This event occurs every May in New York City, just after spring sweeps.

Video On Demand (VOD) Technology that allows viewers to choose video content and have it sent directly to their television.

vision mixer A device used to select between and combine different video sources.

wages Compensation for work performed, usually paid by the hour or by production and delivered weekly or daily to workers such as manual or skilled workers, as opposed to a salary.

workers' compensation A system of benefits provided by employers to employees who are injured on the job, intended to prevent employees from filing civil lawsuits against their employers in an attempt to win monetary damages.

Chapter 6

Resources

Associations and Organizations

Professional

Alliance of Motion Picture and Television Producers (AMPTP)
This organization of producers works with the Screen Actors Guild and other labor unions to agree on terms for wages, pensions, health care, and media rights and residuals. (http://www.amptp.org)

American Federation of Television & Radio Artists (AFTRA)
This is the union that represents the interests of performers in broadcast television and radio. Members include broadcast journalists, performers on public television, actors who work on commercials, and voice-over artists. (http://www.aftra.com)

Directors Guild—Producer Training Plan, Assistant Director Training Program If you are interested in producing, you absolutely owe it to yourself to try to get into this training program. The Assistant Directors Training Program recruits participants from all over the United States and turns them into assistant directors. Because assistant directors often move into producing (not directing), this is a great way to get into the field, make contact, and get some experience. Graduates have gone on to do great things. (http://www.trainingplan.org)

International Alliance of Theatrical Stage Employees, Moving Picture Technicians, Artists, and Allied Crafts (IATSE)
The IATSE is the labor union representing television and other

technicians throughout the United States and Canada. It has over 110,000 members, making it the largest labor union in the entertainment industries. In addition to participating in labor negotiations with other entertainment unions, it offers scholarships, works to promote safety, lobbies for legislation, and holds an annual convention for members. (http://www.iatse-intl.org)

Screen Actors Guild This is the Web site of the television and screen actors' union. If you want to be a television actor, you will have to find a way to join either this organization or AFTRA. SAG's Web site is full of useful information for prospective and current members, including articles on compensation, contracts, and sections for new performers (i.e., child actors). (http://www.sag.org)

The Society of Motion Picture and Television Engineers (SMPTE) This is the main organization for engineers, camera operators, technical directors, and editors. It sponsors regular events and conferences, publishes a newsletter, and maintains several committees that work to keep up standards within the industry. (http://www.smpte.org)

Steadicam Operators Association This association provides workshops for steadicam operators, information on gear, and links to producers and jobs. (http://www.steadicam-ops.com/index.shtml)

Writers Guild of America Definitely read the writer's resources! This section is full of articles by successful television writers who generously share their experiences and advice on breaking in and moving up. (http://wga.org)

Jobs and Education

Academy of Art University School of Motion Pictures & Television This school in San Francisco offers courses in acting for television, commercials, and voice-over, cinematography, lighting, digital cinematography, directing, editing, script writing for film and television, special effects, makeup, music videos, and many other topics. Students can earn a BFA or MFA. Graduates have gotten jobs at DreamWorks, Pixar, and a number of other prestigious studios. (http://www.academyart.edu/film-school/index.html)

Directors Guild–Producer Training Plan This Web site provides information about the Assistant Directors Training Program offered jointly by the Directors Guild of America and the Alliance of Motion Picture & Television Producers. The purpose of the program is to train new assistant directors to work in the television and motion picture fields. (http://www.trainingplan.org)

NBC Universal Careers NBC Universal runs many networks, including Bravo, CNBC, MSNBC, NBC Sports, Oxygen, SyFy, 13th Street, and USA. That means the company needs thousands of employees and is constantly hiring. Of particular note to those just entering the field are NBC's internships and its Early Career Programs, which include the page programs made famous by the show *30 Rock*. In addition to posting numerous job opportunities, the Web site also posts advice to job seekers, explaining how to break into industries such as television writing. (http://www.nbcunicareers.com)

Tisch School of the Arts, Undergraduate Film and TV Want to study television in New York? NYU's Tisch School of the Arts in the East Village offers training in all aspects of television production. The program teaches scripts, directing, producing, shooting, editing, acting, sound, art direction, animation, and distribution. Students also take cinema studies and a selection of liberal arts classes. The program is highly selective—put together your best portfolio before applying. (http://filmtv.tisch.nyu.edu/page/home.html)

Warner Brothers Careers Warner Brothers Entertainment runs a huge number of television operations, including CNN and HBO.

Best
Practice

Networks constantly advertise jobs. Check these job listings at least once a week. Aside from the fact that you may find an advertisement for the perfect job for you, this will give you a sense for what the industry needs, provide you with a feel for the language used in television operations, and help you plot your career moves. You may also notice a job that would be perfect for someone you know. Be sure to pass the information on to that person—you never know when he or she may return the favor.

The company employs about 10,000 people throughout the world, in all areas of expertise—writing, producing, sales, technical, legal, and anything else necessary to the production of television programming. The Web site lists current jobs. Check out opportunities regularly. If you are more interested in getting into the industry than making lots of money right away, you can apply for various unpaid internships, which are a great way of getting your foot in the door. (http://warnerbrotherscareers.com)

Writers on the Verge This program, sponsored by NCB Universal, is a ten-week program designed to get writers ready to work as staff writers for television series. If you have written a script or two and just need some help polishing your work and getting in the door, you should apply to this program. You will have to go to California, but there are worse places to be! (http://www. nbcunicareers.com/earlycareerprograms/writersontheverge .shtml)

UCLA School of Theater, Film and Television If you want to go to college, learn about film and television, and be right there in Los Angeles where the jobs are, you could do worse than attending this school. You can also take summer courses. Alumni have gone on to work in a plethora of high-profile productions. Ever heard of Jack Black, Carol Burnett, or Ben Stiller? They went to UCLA. (http://www.tft.ucla.edu)

USC School of Cinematic Arts USC trains writers, directors, producers, animators, interactive designers, and entrepreneurs within the television and film fields. The school teaches about 1500 undergraduate and graduate students each year. The school also offers open classes for students across USC. (http://cinema.usc.edu)

Books and Periodicals

Books

All You Need to Know About the Movie and TV Business. By Scott Trost and Gail Resnik (Fireside, 1996). This book was written by two entertainment attorneys. It covers the ins and outs of film and television, with emphasis on contracts and the bureaucracy involved in getting shows broadcast. This is a particularly good resource for actors, especially if they work in Los Angeles.

The Complete Make-up Artist: Working in Film, Television and Theatre. By Penny Delamar (Northwestern University Press, 1995).

This book covers several different types of makeup application, including "straight" makeup (i.e., for news announcers who simply want to enhance their own looks) and character makeup along with step-by-step photographs illustrating different principles. It includes profiles of students who have gone into makeup artistry.

Dealmaking in the Film and Television Industry from Negotiations through Final Contracts. By Mark Litwak (Silman-James Press, 2002). This book, written by an entertainment attorney and law professor, is a guide to the laws that currently govern the entertainment world. The legal regime surrounding television is very complex; whether you are an actor, writer, director, or producer, learning as much about the law as possible will be to your advantage.

Directing and Producing for Television: A Format Approach. By Ivan Cury (Focal Press, 2006). If you want an easy-to-read, step-by-step guide to directing or producing a television program, this is a good book for you. It covers a range of show types, mainly shot with multiple cameras, and introduces the reader to all the key players in the television studio.

Documentary Film: A Very Short Introduction. By Patricia Aufderheide (Oxford University Press, 2007). Do you want to make documentaries? This is a great introduction to the field, and a good resource for someone who wants to learn more about the history and philosophy of documentary filmmaking. The author covers several genres of documentary film, including nature films, public affairs films, and government propaganda, and discusses problems of objectivity and bias.

Four Arguments for the Elimination of Television. By Jerry Mander (Harper Perennial, 1978). Okay, if you are working or planning to work in the television field, you probably do not believe television should be eliminated. But you have also probably noticed that many people, among them parents and educators, believe that television is inherently bad for people, especially children. It is always a good idea to understand arguments against your position, and this book is something of a classic in making the case against television. The author worked in advertising for years before writing this book, in which he suggests that television dumbs down information for the masses, limits the flow of real information, and can be used to influence large numbers of people.

How to Write for Television. By Madeline Dimaggio (Fireside, 2008). The author of this book has written a number of television scripts

Fast Facts

For a personal view of working in television, consider reading a memoir or two of an industry veteran. Melissa Gilbert, who starred as Laura Ingalls in *Little House on the Prairie,* published her memoir *Prairie Tales* in 2009. In this book she shares her experience working as a child and her difficult transition to adulthood. Robert Mudd's memoir *The Place to Be: Washington, CBS, and the Glory Days of Television News* provides a thorough look at one man's years working in broadcast journalism. *Eighty Odd Years in Hollywood: Memoir of a Career in Film and Television,* by actor John Meredyth Lucas, describes life in entertainment in the early days of television. Actor Robert Wagner's autobiography, *Pieces of my Heart,* spills secrets about his marriages and raises questions about his sexual orientation. Even in print, television professionals need to provide entertainment, and scandal is known to sell.

for sitcoms, pilots, soaps, one-hour dramas, and television movies. In her book, she addresses such topics as selling a story, developing pilots and episodes, creating characters, adapting books and stories for television, and marketing scripts.

Reading for a Living: How to be a Professional Story Analyst for Film and Television. By Terri Katahn (Blue Arrow Books, 1990). If you can ignore the outdated information about buying word processors and dot matrix printers, the fundamental content of this book is still sound because the processes of reading, writing, and editing scripts do not change nearly as fast as technology. This book is highly recommended for anyone who wants to learn more about what makes a script good and to find work as a script reader, editor, or writer.

Story. By Robert McKee (HarperEntertainment, 1997). If you want to become a television writer, you must read *Story,* considered by many the "bible" of screenwriting. McKee breaks down the process of writing a script into its many components and describing the key principles of classical script construction. He emphasizes the importance of learning the basics of a traditional story before branching out into alternative forms.

Successful Television Writing. By Lee Goldberg and William Rabkin (Wiley, 2003). If you are already writing for television, or hope to break into the field and already know something about it, this book can help you. It explains how a television series works, including concept, characters, and story structure, provides advice on pitching ideas to showrunners, and provides plenty of exercises to allow you to practice your skills. The authors are themselves both successful showrunners and really know the industry.

Television Disrupted: The Transition from Network to Networked TV. By Shelly Palmer (Focal Press, 2006). This book covers the history of television from the formation of the networks to the developed of the "new media," the "networked" television of the title, and comes up with predictions for the possible future of the television field. This is a good book for anyone who currently works in television or who wants to break in, and feels the need to get a handle on the constantly changing landscape.

The Television PA's Handbook. By Avril Rowlands (Focal Press, 1993). Are you interested in becoming a production assistant, or in improving your performance if you already are one? This book is a great introduction to the field, describing the daily activities of a PA and outlining various types of television production.

Television Production Handbook. By Herbert Zetti (Wadsworth Publishing, 2008). This textbook, written by a television insider, clearly explains the three major phases of television production. It has been updated to include digital production techniques.

The Television Will be Revolutionized. By Amanda Lotz (NYU Press, 2007). Can you predict what television will become in the next generation? Not many people can, but Lotz does a good job of analyzing where television has been and how it is likely to evolve in the near future. The fundamental business model on which network television grew up in the twentieth century has been changed as a result of technological innovation, new forms of advertising, and precisely targeted cable channels. Lotz interviews industry professionals, attends conferences, and examines popular shows to show how television is changing.

This Business of Television. By Howard J. Blumenthal and Oliver R. Goodenough (Billboard, 2006). If you are interested in producing, writing, or becoming a network executive, this book has good information for you. It covers contracts, television associations, government agencies that oversee broadcasting, network distribution, advertising, new technology, and the financial systems that support television and video entertainment. The authors are an entertainment lawyer and law professor and a television producer.

The TV Writer's Workbook: A Creative Approach to Television Scripts. By Ellen Sandler (Delta 2007). Sandler, a television writer and producer who has worked on the shows *Everybody Loves Raymond* and *Coach*, shares her strategies for writing for television. This handbook includes exercises, script breakdown charts, and sample scripts from hit television shows.

Writing the TV Drama Series: How to Succeed as a Professional Writer in TV. By Pamela Douglas (Michael Wiese Productions, 2007). Television writer Douglas offers many details about the process of writing television drama series. This book covers the unique characteristics of the television series medium, the American script-writing system, and provides advice on how to create your own episodes and sell them to producers. Douglas includes a four-act grid to use to create your own story. Each chapter includes an interview with a television writer, and the book concludes with interviews with Douglas' own former students, several years after they studied with her.

Writing TV Sitcoms. By Evan S. Smith (Perigee Trade, 1999). Do you want to write sitcoms? Consult this book for advice on how the business works, how to find an agent, how to write scripts for the different sitcom formats, and to read tips from writer-producers who have worked on successful shows.

Periodicals

Entertainment Weekly This is a weekly magazine that covers television, film, music, books, theatre, and other forms of entertainment. It targets a general audience of consumers and viewers. The magazine covers celebrity gossip, television ratings, production costs, and other in-depth topics related to the production of entertainment. Many of its articles take the form of reviews of television shows and other productions. The Web site is updated daily with new content. (http://www.ew.com)

Mediaweek This magazine covers the television industry, including the business side of the field. Visit the Web site to find out about the latest ratings, premiere dates, seasonal lineups, and all other news of interest to industry professionals. (http://www.mediaweek.com)

Everyone
Knows

Casting services are often the key to matching talent with jobs. If you want to work on screen, you will need some sort of representation to help you succeed. There are tons of casting services and agents in Los Angeles, New York, and parts in between. A few examples, all in California, include:

Uncut Casting Services, http://www.launcut.com, in Los Angeles.

Cut Above Casting Service, http://www.cutabovecasting.com, in Los Angeles.

Networks Casting Service, http://www.networkscasting.com, in Burbank.

This list is not meant to be a recommendation for any of the listed agencies; be sure to do your own research before contacting any of these services.

People This weekly magazine, with a circulation of nearly 4 million, covers celebrity gossip mixed with human-interest stories. It does not specifically or exclusively cover the television industry, but enough of its content relates to television that it is worth reading at least occasionally. Where else would you find out that one of the hosts of *Dancing with the Stars* is pregnant before she announces the news on her own show? (http://www.people.com)

TV Guide For years television watchers have relied on *TV Guide* to tell them what shows are scheduled for the coming week and to give them the latest gossip on television celebrities. The magazine is still one of the biggest sellers in the United States, but now it's also on the Internet. If you are truly interested in television, you could do a lot worse than visiting this Web site regularly to keep your finger on the pulse of the television world. (http://www.tvguidemagazine.com)

Variety This weekly trade magazine has been published since 1905, when it covered vaudeville. In the 1930s it extended its coverage to the motion picture industry, and later added television, all with a slant toward entertainment industry executives and insiders. Today it's still a good source of industry gossip and glossy tabloid pictures of celebrities. (http://www.variety.com)

Web Sites

Digitalmediawire This Web-based periodical keeps up with developments in digital media. It's focused at executives who work in television, music, computers, or any other field that uses digital media and needs to keep up with current technology. (http://www.dmwmedia.com)

Federal Communications Commission (FCC) The Web site of the federal government's communications-regulating agency is full of information on the history of communications, rules and standards, and explanations of how the agency works and what it does. This is a good place to go if you are confused about the niceties of obscenity and profanity, which the FCC regulates on behalf of American television viewers. (http://www.fcc.gov)

Internal Revenue Service (IRS) No, this is not directly related to careers in television, but if you do go into this field you may find that your tax situation is somewhat unusual and complicated, especially if you earn a lot of self-employment income. The IRS Web site has lots of information that can help you figure out your tax status and what forms you will need to submit. (http://www.irs.gov)

Museum of Broadcast Communications (MBC) The MBC is a nonprofit in Illinois dedicated to collecting, preserving, and presenting historic and contemporary television and radio programming. It maintains archives of programs and offers free access to its content to users everywhere. The collection contains over 100,000 hours of television and radio programs. As of January 2009, about 7,000 hours of this content had been digitized and was available online. The museum also has a physical location in downtown Chicago. (http://www.museum.tv)

Index

A

AAP. *See* affirmative action plan
ABC. *See* American Broadcasting
    Company
Academy of Art University School
    of Motion Pictures & Television,
    118
accommodation, 101
account executive, 55
acting, 86–90
    agents, 85–86, 88, 92, 101
    auditions, 88–89, 102
actors, 70–71
    bit part, 103
    character, 105
    supporting, 115
    training/education for, 87–88
    unions for, 45
AD. *See* assistant director
ADA. *See* Americans with
    Disabilities Act
ADEA. *See* Age Discrimination in
    Employment Act of 1967
administrative/management jobs,
    54, 55–63
    account executive, 55
    assistant director, 55–56, 89
    casting director, 56
    floor manager, 56–57
    general manager/station
        manager, 57
    line producer, 60, 110
    location manager, 60, 110
    location scout, 60–61, 110
    market research analyst,
        57–58
    news director, 58
    news writer, 58
    producer, 58–59, 84–86
    production assistant, 61, 113
    production coordinator, 59–60
    researcher, 61–62
    showrunner/executive
        producer, 62, 114
    statistics person, 62
    television writer, 39, 62–64,
        84–86, 94, 95, 115, 118,
        121–123
ADR. *See* automated dialogue
    replacement
advancement. *See* career
    advancement
advertising, 24, 39
    commercials and, 7, 24, 34,
        106
    infomercials and, 34, 109
    job, 119
    technology and, 43
    television history and, 6–7
    VCR technology and, 3
affirmative action plan (AAP), 101
AFTRA. *See* American Federation
    of Television and Radio Artists
age concerns, 83–84
Age Discrimination in
    Employment Act of 1967
    (ADEA), 101
agents, 85–86, 88, 92, 101
air time, 101
*All You Need to Know About the
    Movie and TV Business* (Trost/
    Resnik), 120
Alliance of Motion Picture and
    Television Producers (AMPTP),
    117
American Broadcasting Company
    (ABC), 8–9, 42
American Federation of Television
    and Radio Artists (AFTRA), 45,
    117

Americans with Disabilities Act
(ADA), 101
AMPTP. *See* Alliance of Motion
Picture and Television Producers
anchor, news, 71
    career advancement for, 92–93
    non-compete agreements and,
    100
animation, 101
    claymation, 105
announcer, 71
    career advancement for, 92–93
    non-compete agreements and,
    100
annual staffing season, 85
aperture, 102
art department, 102
art department coordinator,
    interview with, 96–97
art director production designer,
    63–64
artistic jobs, 63–70
    art director production
    designer, 63–64
    background artist, 102
    colorist, 64, 106
    continuity director, 64
    director, 64–65, 107
    director of photography (DP)
    cinematographer, 65
    editor, 65–66
    foley artist, 66
    graphic designer, 66
    hair stylist, 66–67
    key makeup artist, 67
    key wardrobe/costume
    supervisor, 67
    lighting director, 68
    makeup artist, 73
    makeup effects artist, 68–69
    props master, 69, 113
    set director, 70
    wardrobe assistant/costumer,
    70

aspect ratio, 102
assistant(s), 69, 84, 89
    assistant director (AD), 55–56,
    89
    production, 61, 113
    wardrobe, 70, 106
assistant director (AD), 55–56, 89
associations/organizations
    jobs/education, 118–120
    professional, 117–118
at-will employees, 99, 102
auditions, 88–89, 102
    cattle call, 104
Aufderheide, Patricia, 121
automated dialogue replacement
    (ADR), 102
Avatar, 90
axis of action, 102

B

background artist, 102
backlot, 102
behind-the-scenes jobs, career
    advancement for, 93–96
Bell, Alexander Graham, 1
benefits, 28, 112, 116
best boy, 74, 102
billing, 102
bit part, 103
black and white, 103
blacklisting, 103
blocking, 103
blooper, 103
bluescreen, 103
Blumenthal, Howard J., 123
body double, 103, 104
books, 120–124
    memoirs, 122
boom microphone, 103
boom operator, 103
bounce board, 103
breakdown script, 103
broadcasting
    cable, 24, 42–44

categories in, 23
current trends in, 34–36
electronics and, 4–5
employment in television v.
 radio, 23
employment statistics, 24
future trends in, 36–39
licensing, 10–11
part-time employment in, 25
broadcast journalism, 29
broadcast networks, major,
 41–42

C

cable broadcasting
 coaxial, 4–5
 employment statistics, 24
 networks, 42–44
cable puller, 74–75
call, 103
call sheet, 103
cameo, 103
camera control unit (CCU), 105
camera control unit (CCU)
 operator, 75
camera crew, 103
camera operators, 32, 75–76
career advancement, xiv. *See also*
 success
 acting and, 86–90
 behind-the-scenes job, 93–96
 entry-level positions and, 35,
  59, 87, 95–96
 extras and, 89–90
 on-screen job, 86–93
 producer/director, 84–86
 television writer, 84–86
cast, 104
casting agencies/services, 104,
 125
casting calls, 88–89, 91–92, 104
casting director, 56
caterer, 104
cathode ray, 1

cattle call, 104
CBS. *See* Columbia Broadcasting
 System
CCU. *See* camera control unit
censorship, 105
CGI. *See* computer generated
 imagery
character actor, 105
chief engineer, 76
chief lighting technician. *See*
 gaffer/chief lighting technician
choreographer, 105
chroma key, 105
chronology, television history,
 20–22
chyron, 105
cinematographer, 65
cinematography, 105
clapper, 105
claymation, 105
clean take, 105
cliffhanger, 105
closed captioning, 40, 105
Coach, 124
coaxial cable, microwave v., 4–5
COBRA. *See* Consolidated
 Omnibus Budget Reconciliation
 Act of 1986
color
 temperature, 106
 timing, 106
colorist, 64, 106
colorization, 106
color television, 12
Columbia Broadcasting System
 (CBS), 8, 14, 42, 50
comedies, situation, 31–32
commercials, 7, 24, 34, 106
commercial television, funding
 for, 24
Communications Act of 1934,
 48–49, 106
compensatory (comp) time,
 106

competition
    employment, 34–35, 36–37
    FCC and, 49–50
The Complete Make-up Artist:
    Working in Film, Television and
    Theatre (Delamar), 120–121
composite, 106
computer generated imagery
    (CGI), 105
Consolidated Omnibus Budget
    Reconciliation Act of 1986
    (COBRA), 105–106
continuity, 106
continuity director, 64
contractor, independent, 109
controversial programming, 18
costume, 106
    supervisor, 67
costumer, 70, 106
crane shot, 106
creator, 106
crew, 106
Cury, Ivan, 121
cut, 106
Cut Above Casting Service, 125
cutting room floor, 57, 106
CW network, 42

D
daytime drama, 106
Dealmaking in the Film and Television
    Industry from Negotiations through
    Final Contracts (Litwak), 121
Delamar, Penny, 120–121
Department of Labor, 107
depth of field, 107
develop, 107
d-girl, 59
dialogue, 107
Digitalmediawire, 126
digital technology, 36, 126
    satellite, 19
    television and, 40
Dimaggio, Madeline, 121–122

Directing and Producing for Television:
    A Format Approach (Cury), 121
director(s), 64–65, 107
    assistant, 55–56, 89
    casting, 56
    continuity, 64
    lighting, 68
    local initiatives, interview
        with, 16–18
    news, 58
    set, 70
    technical, 78
    videotape, 79
director of photography (DP)
    cinematographer, 65
Directors Guild of America, 45
Directors Guild-Producer Training
    Plan, 117, 118–119
discrimination, 107
dissolve, 107
distribution, television shows,
    12–13
documentaries, 30, 107, 121
Documentary Film: A Very Short
    Introduction (Aufderheide), 121
Dolan, Charles, 14
dolly, 107
dope sheet, 107
double
    body, 103, 104
    stunt, 104
Douglas, Pamela, 124
DP. *See* director of photography
dramas, 30
dresser, 107
dubbing, 107
DuMont, 9
DVDs, 22
DVR, 107

E
The Ed Sullivan Show, 6
edit, 107
editor, 65–66

education. *See* training/education
educational programming, 10
electrician/lighting technician,
   76
electronics, broadcasting and,
   4–5
employee, 108
   at-will, 99, 102
employment
   benefits, 28, 112, 116
   competition, 34–35, 36–37
   contract, 108
   education resources and,
      118–120
   entry-level positions, 35
   freelance, 28, 85
   hours/working conditions,
      26–27, 97, 98
   intermittent, 96–100
   job advertising and, 119
   location and, 81–82
   motion picture industry,
      25–26
   part-time, 25
   staffing season and, 85
   statistics, 24–26
   television v. radio, 23
   unions for specific types of, 45
   wages/salaries and, 25, 27–28
engineer. *See* technician/engineer
entertainer, 72
Entertainment Weekly, 124
entry-level positions, 35, 59, 87,
   95–96
   television writer, 95
episode, 108
ethics, strikes and, 38
Everybody Loves Raymond, 124
executive producer. *See*
   showrunner/executive producer
exempt/exemption, 108
exposition, 108
exterior, 108
extra, 72, 89–90, 108

F
fade, 108
Fair Labor Standards Act (FLSA),
   108
Family and Medical Leave Act
   (FMLA), 108
FCC. *See* Federal Communication
   Commission
Federal Communication
   Commission (FCC), 9, 108, 126
   cable restrictions by, 13
   digital technology policy of,
      19
   establishment of, 10–11
   freeze by, 11
   issues of law/regulation and,
      49–51
   obscenity laws of, 51–52
federal communications laws,
   48–49
flashback, 108
flexible spending account (FSA),
   109
floor manager, 56–57
FLSA. *See* Fair Labor Standards Act
FMLA. *See* Family and Medical
   Leave Act
focus, 108
focus group, 108
foley artist, 66
foreign correspondent, 72–73
*Four Arguments for the Elimination of
   Television* (Mander), 121
401(k), 101
FOX, 42
freelance employment, 28, 85, 108
FSA. *See* flexible spending account
funding, commercial television, 24
Future of Television, 48

G
gaffer, 109
gaffer/chief lighting technician,
   76–77

game shows, 30–31, 92
general manager/station manager,
　57
Goldberg, Lee, 122–123
Goodenough, Oliver R., 123
grammar, 82
graphic designer, 66
greenscreen, 109
grip, 77, 109
　key, 110

H
hair stylist, 66–67
HBO. *See* Home Box Office
HDTV. *See* high definition
　television
head shot, 109
Health Insurance Portability and
　Accountability Act (HIPAA),
　109
hierarchies, television industry, 69
high definition television (HDTV),
　40–41
HIPAA. *See* Health Insurance
　Portability and Accountability
　Act
history
　color television, 12
　technology development, 11–13
　television industry, 1–22
　transmission technology, 1–2
Home Box Office (HBO), 14
Hoover, Herbert, 2
host, 73, 109
hours/working conditions, 26–27,
　97, 98
How to Write for Television
　(Dimaggio), 121–122

I
I Love Lucy, 8
I.A.T.S.E. *See* International
　Alliance of Theatrical Stage
　Employees, Moving Picture

Technicians, Artists and Allied
　Crafts
indecency, 109
independent contractor, 109
individual retirement account
　(IRA), 109
　SEP IRA, 114
industry. *See* television industry
infomercials, 34, 109
insurance, unemployment, 116
interior, 109
intermittent employment, 96–100
Internal Revenue Service (IRS),
　126
International Alliance of
　Theatrical Stage Employees,
　Moving Picture Technicians,
　Artists and Allied Crafts
　(I.A.T.S.E.), 45, 117–118
internship, 95
interviews
　art department coordinator,
　　The Office, 96–97
　local initiatives director, 16–18
　media specialist, 46–47
　property master, 90–91
IRA. *See* individual retirement
　account
IRS. *See* Internal Revenue Service

J
job descriptions, 54–79. *See
　also* career advancement;
　employment
　administrative/management
　　jobs, 54, 55–63
　artistic, 63–70
　extra, 72
　on screen, 70–74
　technical, 74–79, 109, 110, 118
journalism
　broadcast, 29
　pioneer television, 16
　videotape and, 17

K
Katahn, Terri, 122
Keogh plan, 110
key grip, 110
key makeup artist, 67
key wardrobe/costume supervisor, 67

L
laws/regulations, 48–53
    federal communications, 48–49
    obscenity, 51–52
lawsuit, "wardrobe malfunction," 50
layoff, 110
layout, 110
lead, 110
licensing, broadcast, 10–11
light board, 110
lighting, 110
lighting department, 110
lighting director, 68
lighting technician/electrician, 76
lined script, 110
line producer (unit production manager), 60, 110
Litwak, Mark, 121
live area, 110
local affiliate, 110
location, 110
    manager, 60, 110
    scout, 60–61, 110
location, employment, 81–82
Los Angeles, 81–82
Lotz, Amanda, 123
lower third, 110
lyrics, 110

M
makeup, 110
makeup artist, 68, 73
    key, 67
    makeup effects artist, 68–69

management jobs. *See* administrative/management jobs
Mander, Jerry, 121
market research analyst, 57–58
"mature content" rating, 52
MBC. *See* Museum of Broadcast Communications (MBC)
McKee, Robert, 122
Mediaweek, 124
memoirs, 122
microphone, boom, 103
microwave transmission, coaxial cable v., 4–5
mini-series, 111
minorities, in television industry, 17–18
mise-en-scène, 110
mixing console, 111
montage, 111
motion capture, 111
motion picture industry, 24, 25
    employment in, 25–26
Museum of Broadcast Communications (MBC), 126
music supervisor, 111

N
NAB Show, 48
National Association of Radio and Television Broadcasters, 6
National Broadcasting Company (NBC), 7–8, 41
NATPE Convention, 48
NBC (National Broadcasting Company), 7–8
NBC Universal Careers, 119
network, 112
networking, viii, xiv, 91
    advertising through social, 43
    success through, 81–84
networks, broadcast
    cable/satellite, 42–44
    history of development, 7–8

job advertising by, 119
major, 41–42
program timing and, 28–29
Networks Casting Service, 125
new media, 37
New York City, 81–82
news, history and, 18
news anchor, 71
career advancement for, 92–93
non-compete agreements and, 100
news director/writer, 58
Nielsen ratings, 111–112
Nipkow, Paul, 2
non-compete agreements, 100, 112

O
obscenity, 51–52, 112
off-book state, 112
The Office, 96–97
on-screen jobs, 70–74
actor, 45, 70–71, 105, 115
anchor, 71, 92–93, 100
announcer, 71, 92–93
career advancement for, 86–93
entertainer, 72
extra, 72
foreign correspondent, 72–73
host, 73
reporter, 73–74
outsourcing, 36–37
outtake, 112
overtime, 98, 112
premium pay for, 112–113

P
PA. *See* production assistant
paid leave, 112
Palmer, Shelly, 123
pan, 112
pan and scan technique, 112
Paramount, 9
parental guidelines, 52–53
part-time employment, 25

PBS. *See* Public Broadcasting System
People, 124–125
periodicals, 124–125
photophone, 1
physical fitness, 32
pixelate, 112
point of view (POV), 112
pornography, 112
postproduction, 112
postwar boom, television industry history and, 5–7
POV. *See* point of view
premium pay, 112–113
premium television, 113
prime time, 113
producer, 58–59, 84–86
Producers' Guild, viii
producing/directing, 84–86
production, 113
production assistant (PA), 61, 113
production coordinator, 59–60
production designer, art director, 63–64
profanity, 113
professional associations/organizations, 117–118
programming. *See* shows/programming
prop, 113
property master, interview with, 90–91
props master, 69, 113
prosthetic, 113
Public Broadcasting System (PBS), 42
publicist, 113
punctuality, 82
puppeteer, 113
pyrotechnics, 113

R
Rabkin, William, 122–123
radio, 6

employment in television v.,
  23
Radio Corporation of America
  (RCA), 3–4, 7–8
radio waves, 11
ratings
  Nielsen, 111–112
  television show, 52–53
RCA (Radio Corporation of
  America), 3–4, 7–8
*Reading for a Living: How to be a
Professional Story Analyst for Film
and Television* (Katahn), 122
reality television/shows, 31, 35, 39,
  91–92
reasonable accommodation, 113
regulations
  laws and, 48–53
  obscenity, 51–52
religious television programming,
  52
reporter, 73–74
rerun, 113
researcher, 61–62
Resnik, Gail, 120
resources
  agent, 85
  associations/organizations,
    117–120
  books, 120–124
  periodicals, 124–125
  training/education, 87–89,
    93–94, 118–120
  Web sites, additional, 125, 126
retirement, 98–99
  401(k) plan for, 101
Rowlands, Avril, 123

S
safe area, 113
safe harbor, 51, 113
SAG. *See* Screen Actors Guild
salary. *See* wages/salaries
Sandler, Ellen, 124

satellite transmission, 15, 18–19
  digital, 19
  networks, 42–44
scene, 114
score, 114
scout, location, 60–61, 110
Screen Actors Guild (SAG), 45, 71,
  118
screen tests, 88–89, 114
script, 114
  breakdown, 103
  lined, 110
  spec, 85, 115
segment producer, 63
SEP IRA, 114
serial, 114
series, 114
  mini-, 111
set, 114
set director, 70
sexual harassment, 114
shoot, 114
shooting script, 114
shot, 114
showrunner/executive producer,
  62, 114
shows/programming
  controversial, 18
  distribution of, 12–13
  early television, 5–6
  educational, 10
  game, 30–31, 92
  miniseries, 111
  reality, 31, 35, 39, 91–92
  religious, 52
  rerun, 113
  timing of, 28–29
  types of, 29–34
  videotape recording of,
    12–13
sitcom, 114
situation comedies, 31–32
sketch, 114
Smith, Evan S., 124

SMPTE. *See* The Society of Motion Picture and Television Engineers
soap operas, 32–33, 106, 115
social networking, 43
The Society of Motion Picture and Television Engineers (SMPTE), 118
sound engineer. *See* sound operator/sound engineer
sound operator/sound engineer, 77
speaking role, 115
spec script, 85, 115
sports events, 33
staffing season, annual, 85
stand-in, 115
station, 115
statistics
    employment, 24–26
    wages/salaries, 25, 27–28
statistics person, 62
steadicam, 115
steadicam operator, 77–78, 118
Steadicam Operators Association, 118
stock footage, 115
Story (McKee), 122
strikes
    ethics of, 38
    Television Writers Strike of 2007–2008, 35–36
studio, 115
stunt double, 104
success, 80–100
    networking for, 81–84
    six keys to, 80
Successful Television Writing (Goldberg/Rabkin), 122–123
supporting actor, 115
sweeps, 115
syndication, 115

T
take, 115
talk shows, 33

taxes, 99–100
TD. *See* technical director
technical director (TD), 78
technical jobs, 74–79
    best boy, 74, 102
    cable puller, 74–75
    camera operators, 75–76
    chief engineer, 76
    electrician/lighting technician, 76
    gaffer/chief lighting technician, 76–77
    grip, 77, 109, 110
    sound operator/sound engineer, 77
    steadicam operator, 77–78, 118
    technical director, 78
    technician/engineer, 78
    videotape director, 79
    videotape operator, 79
technician/engineer, 78
technology
    advertising and, 43
    closed captioning, 40
    digital, 19, 36, 126
    digital satellite, 19
    digital television, 40
    DVD, 22
    HDTV, 40–41
    important, 40–41
    satellite transmission, 15, 18–19, 42–44
    television industry history, 11–13
    transmission, 1–2, 4–5, 11, 15, 18–19, 42–44
    twenty-first-century, 19–20
    V-chip, 52–53
    VCR, 3
    videotape, 12–13, 17
Telecommunications Act of 1996, 49
telectroscopes, 1

television. *See also* television
industry
  advertising and, 6–7
  black and white, 103
  color, 12
  digital, 40
  early, 5–6
  high-definition, 40–41
  parental guidelines, 52–53
  pioneer journalism in, 16
  premium, 113
  prime time, 113
  ratings, 52–53, 111–112
  reality, 31, 35, 39
  religious programming on, 52
Television Code, 6
*Television Disrupted: The Transition
from Network to Networked TV*
(Palmer), 123
television industry, xiii–xiv.
  See also broadcasting; job
  descriptions
  advertising and, 6–7, 24
  age and, 83–84
  broadcast networks in, 7–8,
    28–29, 41–44, 119
  cable/satellite networks in,
    42–44
  chronology, 20–22
  decline of, 39
  early television, 2–5
  events in, 48–53
  hierarchies within, 69
  history of, 1–22
  intermittent employment in,
    96–100
  minorities in, 17–18
  modern developments in,
    19–20
  network development in, 7–8
  new media in, 37–39
  opportunities in, 47
  pioneer journalism in, 16
  postwar boom and, 5–7

  price of first TVs and, 4
  terminology jargon in, xiv
  women in, 17–18
The Television PA's Handbook
(Rowlands), 123
Television Production Handbook
(Zetti), 123
The Television Will be Revolutionized
(Lotz), 123
television writers, 62–64, 118,
121–123
  career advancement, 84–86
  entry-level positions for, 95
  reality, 39
  spec scripts and, 85, 115
  training/education, 94
Television Writers Strike of 2007-
2008, 35–36
This Business of Television
(Blumenthal/Goodenough), 123
timeshifting, 115
Tisch School of the Arts,
  Undergraduate Film and TV, 119
trade secret, 115
training/education
  actors, 87–88
  assistant directors, 89
  associations/organizations,
    118–120
  behind-the-scenes jobs and,
    93–94
  writers', 94
transmission technology
  coaxial cable v. microwave,
    4–5
  1800s, 1–2
  mechanical, 2
  satellite, 15, 18–19, 42–44
  VHF/UHF, 11
trends
  broadcasting, 34–36
  future, 36–39
Trost, Scott, 120
TV-14 rating, 53

TV-G rating, 53
TV Guide, 125
TV-MA, 53
TV-PG rating, 53
The TV Writer's Workbook: A Creative Approach to Television Scripts (Sandler), 124
TV-Y rating, 53
TV-Y7, 53
type, 115
typecasting, 116

U
UCLA School of Theater, Film and Television, 120
UHF (ultra high frequency), 11
Uncut Casting Services, 125
unemployment insurance, 116
unions, xiii, 28, 44–48, 83, 98. *See also* strikes
    for specific employment, 45
United Scenic Artists, 45
unit production manager. *See* line producer
upfront, 116
USC School of Cinematic Arts, 120

V

Variety, 125
V-chip, 52–53
VCRs, advertising and, 3
VHF (very high frequency), 11
video editor, 65–66
Video on Demand (VOD), 41, 43, 116
video production industry, 24, 25
    employment statistics, 26–27
videotape, 12–13
    journalism and, 17
videotape (VT) director, 79
videotape (VT) operator, 79
vision mixer, 116

VOD. *See* Video on Demand
VT. *See* videotape (VT) director; videotape (VT) operator

W
wages/salaries, xiii, 114, 116
    age and, 83
    premium pay, 112–113
    statistics on, 25, 27–28
wardrobe assistant/costumer, 70, 106
"wardrobe malfunction" lawsuit, 50
wardrobe/costume supervisor, key, 67
Warner Brothers Careers, 119–120
War of the Worlds (Wells), 14
WDSU, 16
Web sites, 126
    casting agencies/services, 125
Wells, H.G., 14
Western Union, 5
WGA. *See* Writers Guild of America
women, in television industry, 17–18
workers' compensation, 116
writers, 38, 121–122
    news, 58
    older, 83
    reality television and, 39
    segment, 63
    strike by, 35–36
    television, 35–36, 62–64, 84–86, 94, 95, 115, 121–123
    training/education, 94
Writers Guild of America (WGA), 38, 45–47, 118
Writers on the Verge, 94, 120
Writing the TV Drama Series: How to Succeed as a Professional Writer in TV (Douglas), 124
Writing TV Sitcoms (Smith), 124